IMAGES ACROSS THE AGES
CHINESE PORTRAITS

Dorothy
and
Thomas Hoobler

RSVP
**RAINTREE
STECK-VAUGHN**
PUBLISHERS
The Steck-Vaughn Company

Austin, Texas

Cover and interior design: Suzanne Beck
Illustrations: Victoria Bruck
Electronic Production: Scott Melcer
Project Manager: Joyce Spicer

Library of Congress Cataloging-in-Publication Data
Hoobler, Dorothy.
    Chinese portraits / by Dorothy and Thomas Hoobler : illustrated by Victoria Bruck.
        p.   cm. — (Images across the ages)
    Includes bibliographical references and index.
    Summary: Portraits of people prominent in Chinese civilization over a 3000-year period: Confucius, Shi Huang Di, the Ban family, Empress Wu, Li Bo and Du Fu, Ma Yuan, Zheng He, Yuan Mei, Lin Xezu, and the Soong family.
    ISBN 0-8114-6375-3
    1. China — Biography — Juvenile literature.   [1. China — Biography.]   I. Hoobler, Thomas.   II. Bruck, Victoria, ill.   III. Title. IV. Series : Hoobler, Dorothy. Images across the ages.
DS734.H585   1993
920.051—dc20
[B]   92-13617
                                                                        CIP AC

Printed and bound in the United States by Lake Book, Melrose Park, IL
1 2 3 4 5 6 7 8 9 0 LB 98 97 96 95 94 93

Acknowledgments
Poems in Chapter 5
Reprinted with permission of Twayne Publishers, an imprint of Macmillan Publishing Company, from TU FU by A.R. Davis. Copyright © 1971 by Twayne Publishers, Inc.
Reprinted with permission of Field Translation Series, Oberlin College Press, from Four T'ang Poets, translated by David Young. Copyright © 1980

CONTENTS

INTRODUCTION

CHINA'S
LEGENDARY SUPERHEROES

T he history of China is longer than that of any other nation. It stretches back thousands of years into a legendary time, a Golden Age when the country was ruled by Sage Kings—wise rulers. These legendary rulers performed heroic deeds like the superheroes of today. The Chinese credit them with discovering the tools of civilization.

The first mythical rulers were Fuxi and his sister Nuwa, who had human bodies and dragon's tails. Fuxi taught the ancient Chinese people to build houses, make fishnets, and take care of the six traditional Chinese domesticated animals: horses, cattle, dogs, pigs, chickens, and sheep. Fuxi also taught the Chinese how to write.

Nuwa saved the people from China's first great flood. The Huang He, or Yellow River, in northern China was the site of China's earliest civilization. Its waters made farming possible, but its unpredictable floods earned it the name "China's sorrow." Nuwa used four turtle legs to prop up the sky and five colored stones to patch up the holes in the heavens. Then she cleaned up the earth by channeling the waters of the rivers so they would flow smoothly.

A third ruler, Shen Nong, taught the Chinese people about agriculture and medicine. He developed the plow and showed them which soils were good for each crop. Shen Nong carried a healing wand and searched for herbs that could be used for medicines. Because Shen Nong could see through the skin over his stomach, he could learn which herbs were good by watching how they affected his body.

Another Sage King, known as "the Yellow Emperor," conquered the different tribes in the Yellow River region and founded the first Chinese state. He lived in a palace with his court much as later Chinese rulers would do. The court included an astronomer-historian who built an observatory to study the heavens. By watching the phases of the moon, he invented a calendar.

One spring day the Yellow Emperor's wife noticed silkworm cocoons on the mulberry trees in the palace garden. Delighted by the fine strands, the empress had her handmaidens soak the cocoons in water. When she dipped in her comb to stir the cocoons, the silk threads stuck to it. By twisting the comb as she removed it from the water, the empress spun the first silk thread. Silk became one of China's most precious products, and the Empress was honored as the patroness of the industry.

The last of the superhero rulers was Yu, the Great Engineer. He found a way to control the floods that still plagued China. Yu studied the shape of the land before deciding to build canals and dig new beds for the rivers. He worked so tirelessly that he did not see his family for thirteen years. Once he was within sight of his home but passed it by, for his task was more important.

We can see how important water management was to China by looking at the Chinese character for "law." In the written Chinese language, each character makes up a single word. Some characters are very complicated and combine other characters to make a new one. "Law" is made up of the character for "water" and the character for "go." For it was the responsibility of the ruler to make the water go to control the rivers so that the Chinese could grow food for themselves.

Earlier Sage Kings had picked the most able men in the kingdom to be their successors. But Yu named his son to succeed him. He thus began the first dynasty, or ruling family, in Chinese history. By tradition, this Xia Dynasty ruled China from 2100 B.C. to 1600 B.C. The Xia Dynasty is still shrouded in myth and legend. But we know that the Shang Dynasty that followed it actually existed. Its rulers were no longer legendary superheroes, but real people. The Shang was followed by the Zhou Dynasty, and so on in a succession of dynasties that give a pattern to Chinese history. There are distinct differences between each dynasty—in culture, art, and even in the amount of territory each dynasty controlled. Each dynasty added its own stamp to the great civilization of China, down to the 20th century when the last dynasty fell.

The cycle of each dynasty followed a definite pattern. Usually the founder of a dynasty was a dynamic and powerful person. He provided efficient leadership so that the canals and dikes were maintained and agriculture flourished. In some dynasties, strong military leaders expanded China's territory.

Over time, the dynasties always began to weaken. Less capable rulers came to the throne and their control slipped. Sometimes an event such as the appearance of a comet indicated that Heaven disapproved of the emperor. Natural disasters, such as floods, famines, or earthquakes, were believed to be signs that the emperor had lost the "Mandate of Heaven"—his right to rule. Soon a new leader would arise, often at the head of a rebellion. He would seize control and start a new dynasty.

Over the centuries, Chinese civilization spread south from the Huang He river basin to the Yangzi River area. The Chinese also moved westward as far as the world's highest mountains, the Himalayas. Over the more than 3,000 years of China's history, billions of people have lived within its borders. We will tell the stories of a few of them in this book. They come from many different dynasties over a long period of time. Not all of them were the greatest or most powerful people of their day, but each one played a role in creating the world's oldest continuous civilization.

C H A P T E R 1

THE HIDDEN ORCHID— CONFUCIUS

In the year 551 B.C., a boy was born in eastern China. According to legend, the child's mother had a vision while she was pregnant. She saw five old men leading an animal with a horn in the middle of its forehead and scales all over its body. This Chinese unicorn knelt before her and spit out a piece of jade. On it was an inscription that promised that her awaited child would be a "king without a crown." Soon the mother went to a small cave in a nearby hill to give birth. At the moment the child was born, it is said that dragons guarded the cave, and two female spirits sprinkled the ground with perfumes. From nowhere a stream appeared and miraculously washed the newborn. Heavenly music filled the air, and a voice proclaimed that a holy child had been born.

The child of this legend is known as Kong Fuzi, from his family name Kong and the honorary title Fuzi, which means "Master." Master Kong is known in other countries as Confucius. He is the most influential man in Chinese history. His teachings formed the basis for Chinese government, ethics, and family life for more than two thousand years.

Confucius grew up in the small duchy of Lu, at a time when China was broken up into warring states. The Zhou Dynasty, founded around 1100 B.C., was in the last stages of decline. The Zhou rulers controlled only a small area around the capital of Luoyang. The Son of Heaven, the Chinese title for their ruler, lived there and performed age-old ceremonies. These included sacrifices to Heaven— not a place, but rather the most powerful force in the universe. Through the rituals, the Son of Heaven asked for good weather and prosperity for his people. Only the Son of Heaven could offer these sacrifices for the country as a whole. However, in Confucius' time, the emperors were not as strong and powerful as they would become in later dynasties. Princes and dukes ruled smaller Chinese states, competing for power and sometimes even making war on one another.

Confucius' family had once been members of the nobility. They claimed descent from the kings of the Shang Dynasty. But by the time of his birth, the family had fallen on hard times. When Confucius was three, his father died. His young mother had to raise him on what she could earn by farming a meager strip of land awarded to widows.

The young boy went hunting and fishing and worked at a variety of trades. He also learned to read and write at an academy for young nobles. When he completed his studies, Confucius received the "bonnet of manhood" at a special ceremony for family and friends. "On this excellent, this solemn day," he was told, "the bonnet is placed on your head for the first time. May your childish feelings be banished; act in conformity with your quality as a man grown; may your old age be happy; may your happiness accumulate in splendor."

As a young man, Confucius served his state as Collector of the Grain Tithes—a fancy title for tax collector. Confucius made sure that the peasant farmers turned over to the Duke the correct amount of grain as taxes. He also took care to see that the rice was properly stored so that it could be used when needed.

Even then, Confucius was known for his honesty. "My calculation must be correct, that is all I have to care about," he said. But Confucius saw that other officials were not so honest. Some accepted bribes and swindled the people. Yet he was powerless to change the system.

Discouraged with government, Confucius left his post and began a life of teaching. Wandering from place to place, he soon attracted devoted pupils throughout Lu and other states and founded a school. He gave instruction in the Six Arts of ancient China—rituals, writing, music, archery, chariot driving, and mathematics. By tradition, he had 3,000 students.

Confucius believed that education should be more than learning skills. He tried to teach character as well. He himself was always willing to learn from others, including his own students. He believed that learning, rather than high birth, was the basis for being a true gentleman.

In this spirit, he opened his school to all students regardless of birth, a revolutionary gesture for the time. Teachers in those days had no salaries; their pupils brought gifts, usually of food. Confucius offered to teach anyone "who could bring no better present than a bundle of dried meat." (Today "a bundle of dried meat" is a Chinese phrase for a teacher's pay.) He asked only that his students work hard, think about what he said, and persist in their studies. "If I hold up one corner of a square and a man cannot come back to me with the other three, I won't bother to go over the point again," he said.

Why was Confucius so beloved by his pupils? He followed the virtues that he preached—he was always pleasant and considerate of others. He loved music. He played the lute and often sang to create a joyous mood. He also enjoyed outdoor sports. He swam regularly, and practiced archery and chariot driving. Once when he asked four of his pupils what their ambition was, three answered that they would like to be officials. But the fourth claimed that he would like to swim in the river and enjoy nature. Confucius laughed and said, "You are a man after my own heart." Although he was surrounded by admiring pupils, he would admit that he too could be ignorant. "You think," Confucius said, "I know a great deal? I don't."

Another time a pupil said that he had been asked what kind of person Confucius was. The pupil had not been able to answer. Confucius replied, "Why didn't you say that I am a man who pursues the truth untiringly, and teaches people unceasingly, and who forgets to eat when he is enthusiastic about something, and forgets all his worries when happy...and can never remember that he is growing old?"

While teaching, Confucius developed a philosophy, a system of thought that would help people live properly. Confucius' philosophy tried to answer the question of how to live a useful, harmonious life. Harmony—balance, peace, order—is perhaps the most highly valued of all Chinese virtues.

Confucius looked to the past for his answer. He thought of the early days of the Zhou Dynasty, 500 years before, as a Golden Age. A family from the state of Zhou had overthrown the last Shang king, a corrupt and weak ruler. The new Zhou king soon died, leaving his infant son as his heir. The child's uncle, the Duke of Zhou, took control. The Duke was a wise and skillful ruler, and Confucius regarded him as the model for good government.

To Confucius, the first duty of a ruler was to set an example for his subjects. The Duke of Zhou had been a virtuous man who did not seek power for his own glory, but for the good of all. The duke restored order to the country so that people could live safely and prosper. This was particularly important to Confucius, for he himself lived in a time of disorder, when people suffered because their rulers were quarreling among themselves. His home state of Lu was sandwiched between stronger states, whose soldiers often attacked it.

To Confucius, the way to restore and maintain order was for people to understand their role in life and act accordingly. Confucius expressed this simply as, "Let the ruler be a ruler and the subject a subject; let the father be a father and the son a son." Confucius described five basic relationships in society. They were: ruler/subject, father/son, husband/wife, older brother/younger brother, and friend/friend. The strongest of these was between father and son. The loyalty that a son owed his father came before all others, even loyalty to the ruler. In ancient China a son who insulted his father or harmed him even accidentally was harshly punished, sometimes by death.

Each of these relationships required the correct behavior, or *li*. For example, a person should be humble in the presence of his father, or any superior. Confucius set very precise standards for any contact between subject and ruler. A person approaching the ruler should take the first step with the left foot. But when he withdrew, the right foot should go first.

The idea of *li* extended to everyday behavior, even to dress and food. Confucius himself would not sit on a mat unless it was perfectly straight. Before he ate any meat, it had to be cut into precise squares. At meal times, he would not speak. He wore old-fashioned clothing such as a long-sleeved gown and a forked headdress. These had been fashionable 500 years earlier, at the time of the Duke of Zhou. Confucius never wore the colors purple or red, thinking them too garish.

Even in Confucius' time his emphasis on proper behavior was thought to be too fussy. Some people ridiculed his ideas and peculiar habits, but Confucius felt that proper clothing and actions were the first step to a virtuous life.

However, he knew that *li* had little value if it lacked the proper inner spirit. To Confucius, the most important of all virtues was *ren*, which means benevolence or love. Confucius had his own version of the Golden Rule: "Never do to others what you would not like them to do to you." Confucius believed that a true gentleman lived by a high code of conduct for himself, but did not expect the same high conduct from others. It was the goodness of the person rather than high birth that made a true gentleman. All men could be improved through education.

The highest duty of the gentleman was to offer his services to the government. For in Confucius' view, good government came from having officials who were honorable. He put little faith in laws, which he believed rested on the use of force. It was far better to have good officials set an example that would encourage proper behavior among the subjects.

Confucius was further inspired during a visit to Luoyang, where the Zhou kings still reigned. He visited the mounds where the Son of Heaven made sacrifices to heaven on behalf of the country. He visited the Hall of Light, where the king received his subjects. On its walls were pictures of the Sage Kings and the founders of the Zhou Dynasty. "Here," said Confucius, "we see how the Zhous became great. As in a mirror we read the reason for the present in the past."

According to legend, Confucius met a mysterious person named Laozi while visiting Luoyang. Laozi was the keeper of the royal archives. Tradition holds that he founded the other great Chinese philosophy—Daoism.

Daoists sought to find the Way (the *Dao*) to a good life. But they chose nature as their guide. Daoists taught that people are part of nature and should draw on their own inner power to guide their behavior. Study and learning from books were unnecessary. A Daoist saying is, "Knowledge studies others; wisdom is self-known." Human society and government were artificial and so hindered people's ability to act according to nature

Throughout Chinese history, the two philosophies of Confucianism and Daoism have been dominant forces. Though they seem contradictory, a person could be both a Confucian and a Daoist. Confucianism guided official and social life. But in private life, people followed the Daoist Way. Daoism's influence can be seen in the Chinese love of nature, often expressed through art.

Legend says that Laozi advised Confucius to put aside his excessive ambitions, saying, "None of that is any use to you." But Confucius did not take the advice. It was his deepest wish to become an adviser to a great ruler so that he could put his ideas into practice. Confucius failed to attain a post with the Duke of Lu, so he traveled from state to state, searching for a ruler who would appreciate his ideas.

However, history shows that reformers are rarely popular with those in power. Confucius was no exception. In addition, he had a sharp tongue. He said of one ruler who talked too much, "If this man can be endured, who cannot be endured?" He told another ruler who complained about thieves in his territory that the thieves were only following the ruler's own example of greediness. As a result, Confucius was driven out of two states and attacked in another.

These rejections hurt Confucius. He called himself the "hidden orchid," a man whose talents were wasted and his flowering unknown. As he aged, Confucius saw himself as a failure.

Finally, Confucius gave up his quest for office. He returned to Lu and spent his old age studying and editing ancient Chinese works of poetry and history. His edition of these works became known as the Five Classics, and form a major part of Chinese tradition and thought. He died in Lu at the age of seventy-two.

Nevertheless, his ideas were not forgotten. For three years his disciples observed a period of mourning. They kept alive his teachings and spread them to others. Confucius never wrote down his philosophy, but his students collected his ideas in a book called the *Analects*.

Five hundred years after his death, the ideas of Confucius became the official philosophy of China. Down to the present century, government officials were tested on their knowledge of Confucian thought and the Five Classics.

Neighboring countries, such as Japan, Korea, and Vietnam, adopted Confucianism as part of their own philosophy. Even today, the "Confucian ethic"—desire for education, belief in hard work, and close-knit family life—is an important force in East Asia. People still follow the way of life of Master Kong, who died thinking himself a failure 2,500 years ago.

CHAPTER 2

THE FIRST EMPEROR—
SHI HUANG DI

In the year 227 B.C., the scholar Jing Ke left his home state of Yan on a dangerous mission. He hurried along the road to Xianyang, the capital of the state of Qin. Jing Ke was in danger because Yan was at war with Qin. And the king of Qin, whom he hoped to meet, was a suspicious man, ruthless toward his enemies.

However, Jing Ke was carrying something that he hoped would get him inside the king's palace. It was a box that contained the head of a Qin general who had led a rebellion against the king. Jing also brought a detailed map of his home state of Yan, which was a valuable military secret.

But Jing was no ordinary scholar, nor was he a traitor to his home state. Rolled inside the map was a dagger that had been dipped in poison. Jing's mission was to kill King Cheng.

For twenty years, King Cheng of Qin had been fighting with his neighbors. His ambition was to conquer them all, and his military skill made this a real threat. King Cheng aroused fear and dread even among his own people. An advisor described him as having "the nose of a hornet and large, all-seeing eyes. His chest is like that of a bird of prey and his voice like that of a jackal. He is merciless, with the heart of a tiger or a wolf. Should he achieve his goal of conquering the Empire, we shall all become his slaves." And these were the words of a man who had been generously treated by Cheng!

At first, Jing Ke's plan went well. Although King Cheng's guards carefully searched him, taking his sword, they missed the hidden dagger. The king would not allow anyone with a weapon, not even his own guards, into the hall where he met visitors. Knowing this, Jing planned to kill the king before anyone could come to his aid. Inside the audience hall, Jing revealed his "gift"— the head of the traitorous general. King Cheng asked to see the map. Jing stepped onto the raised platform where the king stood. He swiftly unrolled the map and grasped the dagger. Holding the sleeve of the king's robe, he struck at his heart.

But the king jumped back with such force that his sleeve ripped loose from his gown. He turned and ran. As the others in the room watched in horror, Jing threw the deadly dagger. The king ducked behind a pillar, and the dagger missed. Then the court physician rushed forward and struck Jing with his doctor's bag. Jing fell stunned, and the screams inside the chamber brought the guards running. They beheaded Jing. The action of the court physician changed the course of China's history.

King Cheng had come to the throne of Qin in 246 B.C., when he was only thirteen years old. During the past two hundred years, Qin had continually expanded its borders. Ten years earlier, Qin armies overran Luoyang and forced the last Zhou king from his throne. In the confusion that followed, the rulers of each of China's seven large states tried to gain supremacy over the others and take the title of Son of Heaven.

Li Si, an adviser, encouraged the young king's ambitions. "With the might of Qin and the ability of Your Majesty," Li said, conquering the other states "should be as easy as sweeping dust from the top of a kitchen stove."

In 230 B.C. Cheng began his conquests by overrunning the neighboring state of Han. From then on, Qin armies moved against the rest of the states "as the silkworm devours a mulberry leaf." By the year 221, Cheng had defeated all his enemies except the state of Qi. He invited the king of Qi to his court and promptly threw him into prison, where he starved to death. Now all China was united under Cheng's rule.

To mark the great event, Cheng created a new title for himself—"king" was no longer good enough. He announced, "We are Shi Huang Di, ['the First Emperor'], and our successors shall be known as the Second Emperor, Third Emperor, and so on, for endless generations." His state of Qin (pronounced "chin") was formerly spelled Chin in English, and that is how China got its English name. But Shi Huang Di's subjects, fearing his wrath and swift punishments, called him by another name: the Tiger of Qin.

The emperor set out to live up to his new title. He took some

of the defeated soldiers into his own army. Others were used to carry out the immense projects that Shi Huang Di planned. The first of these was the Great Wall of China.

China had often been invaded by fierce warriors from the north. Through the centuries, a series of walls had been built to try to keep them out. Shi Huang Di ordered his best general, Meng Tian, to connect all these walls into an uninterrupted line more than 1,500 miles long. Meng Tian commanded a work force that at times numbered over one million people.

This mammoth task was completed in an astonishingly short time of ten years. Nothing was allowed to halt its progress. The workers struggled through blizzards, sandstorms, and freezing rain, extending the ten-foot-high wall from the mountains on the eastern seacoast to the deserts on China's western borders. Countless people died building what was called the "largest grave-yard in the world."

The Great Wall became a symbol of China. To the Chinese, it separated two ways of life. The "people of the steppe" to the north were "barbarian" nomads who drank milk and ate with their hands. The Chinese, "the people of the sown," were farmers, avoid-ed eating dairy products, and used chopsticks for their meals.

The Wall was only one of Shi Huang Di's many achievements. With soldiers leading the way, the Qin Empire continued to expand its borders. As more lands fell under Shi Huang Di's control, he ordered Chinese to settle in them. To bring water to these new farms, he built a system of canals and dikes. At the height of his reign, China had spread south to the borders of today's Vietnam.

To govern this vast area, the emperor divided the country into districts and appointed a military and a civil officer to govern each one. Because these officials owed their posts to the emperor, he could count on their loyalty. Just to make sure, a secret third official acted as the emperor's eyes, checking on the other two to make sure they were carrying out his orders.

Within Xianyang, his capital city, Shi Huang Di continually built more palaces to glorify his power. Each time his army conquered a new territory, workers in Xianyang constructed a copy of the defeated ruler's palace. So many palaces were built that it was said that they blocked out the sky.

To help unify his domain, Shi Huang Di ordered the construction of a 4,000-mile-long system of roads. He also adopted a program of standardization. Until this time, each of China's separate states had used different weights and measures. Now Shi Huang Di made them the same for the entire country. The Chinese had also used different kinds of coins. In some areas, iron pieces shaped like knives were used; in others, coins had the shape of a fish. The emperor decreed that henceforth, only round coins with a square hole in the middle would be used. (The hole enabled the coins to be held together in strings, called *cash*.)

Shi Huang Di even decreed exactly how wide the axles of farmers' carts should be. Because the dirt roads were soft, cartwheels made ruts in them. A cart that did not fit into these ruts often had a difficult trip. Now the axles of every cart would be alike—and so would the ruts in the road, making it easier for farmers to bring their goods to market.

Most important of all was the standardization of the characters of the Chinese language. They too had differed from state to state, and new characters were often added. Shi Huang Di's scholars made an official list of each character and its meaning. This was important in a country as large as China. Over time, the spoken language in different regions changed, but communication was possible through the common written language. Even today, though Chinese from different regions cannot always understand each other's speech, the written Chinese characters are the same everywhere. The standards set by Shi Huang Di have preserved a unified culture in China for the 2,200 years since he lived.

The emperor was a tireless worker, full of plans and ideas. His scribes wrote out his orders on bamboo strips tied together by a cord. Every day, they brought him reports from thousands of officials in his far-flung empire. Shi Huang Di bragged that he read more than one hundred pounds of documents a day. At any time, he might jump into his carriage and travel to see for himself what was happening. Usually, these journeys were carried out in secret, so that he could catch lazy or corrupt officials by surprise.

There was a dark side to Shi Huang Di's nature. He resented any criticism or opinions that were different from his own. Li Si, his longtime adviser, encouraged his intolerant attitude. "These scholars," he said, "learn only from the old, not from the new, and employ their learning to oppose our rule and confuse the black-headed people [the Chinese]....Let all historical records but those of Qin be destroyed."

So they were. In the year 213 B.C., Shi Huang Di ordered the destruction of all books of history, literature, and philosophy. The only works that were spared were those on agriculture, divination (predicting the future), technology, and—in gratitude to the doctor who had saved his life—medicine. Throughout the country, the emperor's officials launched a hunt for forbidden books. Only the imperial library was allowed to keep copies of them.

As he grew older, Shi Huang Di became obsessed with death. Two other assassins tried to kill him after he became emperor. Though he again escaped, he was clearly frightened. He brought astrologers and magicians to his court. The astrologers claimed to foretell the future, and the magicians worked on potions to prolong his life. The emperor eagerly listened to the tales of travelers who said they had seen people who had the secret of immortality. He sent expeditions to search for the Blessed Isles that lay somewhere in the eastern sea. In these islands, according to Chinese myth, immortal people lived. But the expeditions he sent never returned.

Still, it was clear that he was aging, like any other man. He lashed out at scholars who criticized him, "saying that I lack virtue.

I have had inquiries made about the scholars in the capital and I find that some of them are spreading vicious rumors to confuse the people." The emperor had 460 scholars buried alive.

He became ever more suspicious and secretive. He built covered walkways between each of his many palaces. Thus, no one could see him as he moved from one to another. Anyone who revealed his whereabouts risked death.

The First Emperor even defied the gods themselves. Once, when he was crossing a river, a storm blew up that nearly capsized his boat. His advisers told him that the guardian god of the river was buried inside a nearby hill. The emperor sent thousands of men to destroy all the trees and grass on the hill, and had it painted bright red, the color that convicts were forced to wear.

But death was the one enemy Shi Huang Di could not defeat. While on an inspection tour of the south with Li Si, he died in the year 210 B.C. Li Si feared that if the news reached the capital, the emperor's eldest son would take command. Li Si favored a younger son, who was weak and easily influenced. So Li Si pretended that the emperor was not dead. Each day, he brought food to the carriage in which the body lay and came forth with orders that the emperor had "given" him. As the imperial party headed for the capital, however, people began to notice a strange smell around the carriage. Li Si filled another cart with rotting fish to cover the odor of the decaying body.

When the emperor's body reached Xianyang, it was buried inside a tomb as grand as any of his other projects. The entire burial place spread over an area of 21 square miles. Thousands of statues of soldiers and horses were buried with the emperor. Archeologists found them and began to uncover them in the 1970s. Each statue was carved to represent a different individual. Originally, they were painted with the bright colors of their uniforms. For more than 2,000 years, they have stood guard over the place where China's First Emperor rests.

The dynasty that Shi Huang Di founded lasted less than ten years after his death. The Chinese people, weary of his enormous work projects, rebelled against his successors. Yet the Chinese have a proverb: "Shi Huang Di is dead, but the Wall still stands." Cruel though he was, his mighty accomplishments continue to influence China down to the present day.

THE TIGERS—THE BAN FAMILY

People traveling along one of the dusty yellow roads of northern China in the year A.D. 60 passed four porters carrying a sedan chair. The chair, resting on two poles that the porters shouldered, resembled a large box. Red curtains shielded the traveler who rode inside.

The red curtains and the red jackets that the porters wore had a special meaning for anyone who saw the chair go by. The color indicated that inside was a young woman on the way to her wedding. She was fourteen-year-old Zhao (her name means "luminous" or "bright"), the daughter of the Ban family. In Chinese fashion, she would write her name as Ban Zhao. Family was the most important thing about a person—as it still is in today's China.

As the chair swayed back and forth between the poles, Ban Zhao must have thought of her beloved family. The Bans had produced noted scholars for generations. While growing up, Zhao had learned to read and write, unusual talents for a girl of her time. Zhao's brothers, the twins Gu and Chao, fondly encouraged their little sister. But females were not allowed to follow the life of a scholar. It was Zhao's destiny to become part of another family and to serve them well. In the ordinary course of events, Zhao might never see her father, mother, or brothers again.

Her family had arranged her marriage through a broker who found a suitable match with the Tsao family. Zhao had no say in the matter. Indeed, she had never even seen her husband-to-be. That morning, she had dressed in the red silk veil and jeweled headdress of a bride. Then she went to the ancestral tablets that held the names of her ancestors. Kneeling before them, she announced that she was joining the Tsao family and asked the spirits to intercede with Heaven to help her perform her duties in her new home.

The journey was long, but at last the porters set the chair down. Zhao waited until her bridegroom tapped on the curtains with a white fan. Then he slid the curtains aside and helped her step out. A servant set aflame a small tuft of dried grass and placed it on the ground. Zhao ran quickly over it, to scare away any evil spirits that might have slipped into the bridal chair.

The groom led Zhao inside his home and the couple bowed to each other. The bridegroom removed her veil and walked with her to the Tsaos' own ancestral tablets to announce her arrival. At a wedding feast, the bride and groom sipped rice wine from the two halves of a gourd. Then the bride poured wine from her cup into his, and he into hers. They were now married. The friends and relatives of the Tsao family toasted them in traditional words: "May you have a hundred sons and a thousand grandsons."

The Chinese word for "wife" is written by combining the characters for "woman" and "broom." This aptly describes the role Zhao was expected to play. As a new wife in the household, she was the humblest person within it. Zhao was expected to serve everyone, to be skillful with needle and thread, to spin silk and weave cloth, and to cook the family meals. She had to rise early and after a hard day's work could not sleep until her husband's parents were settled for the night.

Years later Zhao wrote: "At dawn and at nightfall my heart suffered bitter apprehension." She feared most of all the displeasure of her mother-in-law. A woman's status only rose late in life when her own sons brought wives into the family. Then she could command them like servants, just as she had been treated when she first arrived. Zhao could not complain to her husband for, as Confucius had prescribed, he would have to take his mother's side. Respect for his mother came before his feelings for his wife. If Zhao did not please her husband's family, they might even send her back home, a terrible disgrace.

Zhao worked hard, and in a year or two, she fulfilled her primary duty. She gave birth to a son. Now, Zhao's importance rose. Her husband addressed her proudly as "the mother of my son." A messenger brought the good news to the house of Ban.

Zhao's family traced their ancestry back 700 years. In 604 B.C., a baby was abandoned and left to die in swampland in the southern state of Chu. He was an illegitimate son of the royal family. According to legend, a tigress suckled him until he was rescued by

his grandparents. The child was given the name "Tiger Milk." In the local dialect the word for "tiger" was *ban*. So the descendants of Tiger Milk became known as "The Tigers."

Over the centuries the family migrated north and became prosperous. After the overthrow of the Qin Dynasty, the Han Dynasty took control of China. The Han rulers made Confucianism the official doctrine of the country. They gathered Confucian scholars at their court. At last the "hidden orchid" received his just reward.

Ban family members were among those who were welcomed as scholars at the Han court. One of Zhao's ancestors had received rare and precious books from the emperor, the beginning of the family's vast library.

But it was Zhao's great-aunt who brought fame to the family. Called to the imperial court as a concubine, or mistress, she soon became the favorite of the emperor. Well educated like the rest of her family, she gained respect for her devotion to Confucian principles. In one famous episode, she refused to ride with the emperor in his chariot because that was the role for an adviser, not a wife. In time, another woman replaced her as the emperor's favorite, and Lady Ban left the palace. Her farewell note was a poem in which she compared herself to a fan put away in autumn when it was no longer useful. Even today in China, the term "autumn fan" is used to describe a deserted wife.

Zhao's father, Ban Piao, though his name meant "striped tiger," was really a mild-mannered man. As a youth, he traveled widely and studied. This was a period of upheaval and treachery in China. Wang Mang, an ambitious relative of the empress, usurped the throne and declared himself the new Son of Heaven.

Ban Piao did not believe Wang Mang was the rightful ruler. He acted as an adviser to military leaders who helped to place a new Han emperor on the throne. Wang Mang's rule was a dividing line between what was called "the Former Han" and "the Later Han" dynasties.

For his services, Ban Piao was given a post at the new court, but he soon retired to pursue his studies. He instilled in his children the joys of learning. His great love was history. Among the Chinese, history is held to be very important. Confucius himself was believed to have edited the earliest history of China. History was more than a collection of interesting facts. The past was thought to be a mirror for the present age to learn from. All educated Chinese studied it.

Ban Piao began to write a history of China, using materials from his family's library. However, he died before he was able to finish it. His son Gu took up the task. Gu concentrated on recent times, attempting to write the story of the Former Han Dynasty. Unfortunately, an enemy denounced him to the government, and he was thrown into prison.

Gu's crime was correcting and writing history. Only court officials were allowed to do this, not private citizens. It was a serious matter, for Gu was writing about the ancestors of the ruling family.

Ban Chao, Gu's twin brother, rode to Luoyang to defend him. Chao wrote a petition to the Son of Heaven to explain Gu's writings. The emperor called for Gu's manuscript and read it himself. He was delighted, released Gu from prison, and named him to the staff of the Department of Editing Books.

At first, Gu's career at the court was a brilliant one. He became famous for his poetry and also wrote a treatise on chess, the first known book on the game. Meanwhile, he continued work on the history. But when a new emperor came to the throne, Gu became involved in some political intrigue. In A.D. 92 he was again arrested and thrown into prison. Soon afterward, he died.

Meanwhile, Gu's twin brother Chao had followed a different career. To support his mother, he had taken a job as a copyist in a government department. But his heart was not in the job. One day he put down his writing brush. "If a great man be without any other purpose," he said, "at least he ought to...accomplish an exploit in foreign parts."

Chao got his wish. He obtained a commission as an officer in the imperial army. In A.D. 73 he was sent to Central Asia. China had earlier conquered this western region, which is today's Chinese province of Xinjiang. During the upheavals that brought down the Former Han Dynasty, hostile nomads took control of the region. It was Chao's assignment to regain it.

He faced a difficult task. The vast Tarim Basin in this region is a desert area surrounded by mountains. It was a challenge to maintain a water supply for an army traveling across the burning sands. The nomadic peoples who lived near the region, including Mongols and Turks, were fierce fighters who traveled swiftly on horseback. Chinese called these people "barbarians," a loose term for all foreigners, but especially referring to the nomads who lived beyond the Great Wall.

Nevertheless, the desert region had great economic importance to China. It was a link in the famous trade route called the Silk Road. Camel caravans crossed it, carrying silk—a prized commodity in the West, where the secret of making it was still unknown. In return, China obtained such western products as horses, cattle, and seeds. Coins from the Roman Empire have been found in China, showing that the Silk Road trade eventually extended all the way to Europe.

Chao used his diplomatic skills, presenting gifts to some of the nomadic tribes to make them his allies. Setting one tribe against another was an age-old Chinese tactic. But Chao was ready to use force when he had to. "Only he who penetrates into the tiger's lair," he said, "can carry off the cubs." And even though Chao's forces were outnumbered, his Chinese soldiers carried crossbows, far superior to the ordinary bows and spears of the "barbarians." This fearsome weapon did not appear in Europe until more than a thousand years later.

For almost thirty years, Chao led his soldiers through the Tarim Basin. He brought the oases there under Chinese control. He led the Chinese army as far west as the Caspian Sea. His achievements brought fame, honor, and profit to his family, some of whom became merchants in the Silk Road trade. In the year 91, Chao was appointed Protector General of the Western Territories.

His younger sister Zhao was delighted to hear of her brother's glorious career. She was beginning to carve out a name for herself as well. After her husband died, she returned to the Ban household, perhaps because she longed to have access to her family's library. Now, as a widow, she began to study and write on her own.

Gu had died before completing the history that their father began. When the emperor learned of Zhao's work, he appointed her to a court scholar's post, a very unusual honor for a woman. She worked at the Store Books Pavilion, a library within the palace complex. Finally, she finished the *Han Shu*, or History of the Former Han. It became the model for the dynastic histories that would follow.

The emperor had more work for Zhao. He made her the personal tutor of the young empress, teaching writing, astronomy, and mathematics. Zhao expanded her "school" to include the other young ladies of the court. With them, she may not have been so successful. An inscription on a 19th-century print showing Ban Zhao lecturing a group of noble women, reads: "They were like stones."

Zhao used her growing influence to persuade the emperor to allow her brother Chao to come home at last. Now an old man of seventy, Chao was in poor health. He had petitioned the emperor to recall him, but the emperor was reluctant. However, when Zhao wrote a letter describing her brother's accomplishments, the emperor relented. Chao was showered with honors when he reached the capital in the year 102. He had a joyful reunion with his sister, whom he had not seen in more than forty years. Unfortunately, he died a few months later.

Zhao was now over fifty years old, but her career was not over. She may have witnessed one of China's most remarkable discoveries—paper. Tradition holds that in the year 105 a court official presented the emperor with the world's first sheets of paper. The official had combined "the bark of trees, hemp, rags, and fish nets" to make a new material for writing. Chinese scholars had formerly used their ink brushes on such surfaces as bamboo, silk, and parchment. All of these were expensive or bulky to store. The invention of paper made it possible to produce the countless scrolls that preserved Chinese history, scientific knowledge, poems, paintings, legends, and stories. Paper has played a vital role in the development of China's magnificent civilization.

Zhao herself may have been one of the first to use paper when she wrote *Instructions for Women*. This work described the proper behavior for Chinese women and girls. She began with the words:

"I, the writer, am a lowly person with but a monkey's wit." Being a strong Confucian, Zhao looked to tradition. She felt that women and men had different roles. Women had to obey men and were dependent on them economically.

Zhao described the traditional customs that Chinese followed at the birth of a girl. The baby was placed at the foot of the bed and given a piece of pottery. This showed that the baby was lowly and weak and "should regard it as her primary duty to humble herself before others." The piece of pottery signified that her duty was to work hard. When the girl's birth was announced at the ancestors' tablets, it indicated that as a woman she should ensure that the ancient rites would continue to be observed. Zhao wrote

> These three ancient customs , show a woman's ordinary way of life. Let a woman modestly yield to others; let her respect others; let her put others first, herself last. Should she do something good, let her not mention it; should she do something bad, let her not deny it. Let her bear disgrace; let her even endure [it] when others speak or do evil to her. Always let her seem to tremble and to fear.

These are hardly the words we would associate with a woman of such accomplishments. Yet this was the prevailing view of women's role in traditional China. However, Zhao believed that education would raise women's status. She appreciated the benefits that her own education had brought her. Thus, she included a plea for the education of women: "To teach sons and not to teach daughters—is this not to be blinded?" Her concern was a fitting climax to the career of the woman who was China's foremost female scholar.

The Ban family was one of the most remarkable in Chinese history. They lived in a time of progress and change for the sixty million people who lived in Han China. During the four centuries of Han rule, the Chinese made great achievements in the arts, writing, science, technology, and government. The Han era set a high standard that future Chinese would look back on with pride. Even today, one of the names the Chinese give themselves is, "The men of Han."

CHAPTER 4

THE ONLY FEMALE SON OF HEAVEN—EMPRESS WU

In the year 638, a thirteen-year-old girl named Wu Chao left her home in Shanxi Province. She had been summoned to the emperor's court in Changan, the capital city of the Tang Dynasty. Wu Chao's mother was a widow. She knew she would never see her daughter again and wept at her departure. Wu Chao, it is said, calmly chided her mother, saying, "To be admitted to the presence of the Son of Heaven! How can you tell that means unhappiness?"

Just fifty years earlier, China had been reunited under one ruler for the first time since the fall of the Han Dynasty. The reigning emperor was now Tai Zong, one of China's greatest rulers. Scholars and artists flocked to his capital, bringing glory to the Tang. But Wu Chao had been summoned because the emperor had heard of her remarkable beauty. She would become one of Tai Zong's concubines.

As she passed through one of the four great gates in the massive wall around Changan, Wu Chao saw the largest city in all the world. Over a million people lived there. The streets were wide and straight and the houses bright, with curving, yellow-tiled roofs that extended beyond the walls to keep the buildings shaded and cool in the summer months. In its two great marketplaces, merchants sold goods that had come from as far away as Persia and India.

Dotted among the buildings were many Buddhist temples. Buddhism was a religion that grew out of the teachings of an Indian named Gautama, who had lived about the same time as Confucius. Gautama, born wealthy, had given away his riches to search for inner peace. He sought to free himself from the desires of the world, and through meditation he achieved a state of "enlightenment"—perfection through denial of earthly desires. Gautama thus became the Buddha, "the enlightened one."

Buddha's followers spread his teachings to China during the Later Han Dynasty. After the Han Dynasty fell in the year 220, China experienced more than three centuries of disunity. The years of turmoil brought many converts to the new religion, which promised relief from the cares of the world. Buddhist monks and nuns built monasteries as havens of peace and meditation amid a violent world. By the time of the Tang Dynasty, Buddhism was recognized as one of the Three Great Truths—the other two being Confucianism and Daoism.

Wu Chao's carriage made its way up the Street of the Red Bird, an immense boulevard 480 feet wide. At its northern end lay the second part of Changan: the Imperial City, the government headquarters of China's vast empire. It too had a wall around it, for only those on official business could enter. The penalty just for touching the wall was seventy strokes of a rod.

Guards waved Wu's carriage through, for it was painted vermilion, the color of the emperor's court. Inside the second city, thousands of scholar-officials, scribes, and messengers were hard at work. In immense rooms with marble floors, the emperor held his court. Seated on a throne, he listened as his officials brought countless affairs to his attention. With their advice, he made decisions that affected the sixty million people within his empire.

North of the Imperial City was Wu Chao's destination—the third, and most secret, part of the capital. This was the Palace City, where the emperor lived. It was also known as the Forbidden City, for only members of the emperor's household could enter its walls. These included his children, the empress, the concubines, and servants. The emperor was the only man allowed here. Even his sons, once they had grown to manhood, had to move to palaces outside the Forbidden City.

Wu was made a Concubine of the Fifth Grade. (There were nine grades in all.) An older woman taught her the proper etiquette for serving the emperor. Wu also studied music, literature, and calligraphy, or beautiful writing. The Fifth Grade concubines were known as the "Elegants," but Tai Zong soon had a pet name for his newest concubine—"Beauty Wu."

Life inside the Forbidden City was one of unimaginable luxury. Wu enjoyed rich delicacies and wines served in golden bowls and cups. She had her pick of silken robes, jewels, and perfumes. Servants brought anything she desired. The concubines enjoyed strolling through the palace gardens, sometimes playing games that included polo. Many of the emperor's women spent hours arranging their hair and faces in the latest fashions. Among the fads was painting their eyebrows in different styles, such as "Sorrow Brows" and "Distant Mountains."

But their splendid life would last only as long as the emperor lived. When he died, they would have to leave the court, become Buddhist nuns, and spend the rest of their lives in study and prayer. And, in the year 649, when Wu was just twenty-four years old, Tai Zong lay dying.

Wu had no wish to give up her life in the palace. She saw her chance when the crown prince, Gao Zong, came to visit his father. Wu caught him alone and caused him to fall in love with her. Later writers, hostile to Wu, said she used sorcery and tricks. Probably, it was only that Gao found her as beautiful as his father did.

After Tai Zong's death, Wu obediently followed tradition. She shaved her head and entered a Buddhist convent, hoping that Gao Zong would not forget her.

In fact, it was not Gao but his wife the empress who caused Wu's return to the Palace. The empress was unable to have children. She feared that her husband would replace her with the "Pure Concubine," a beautiful noblewoman. The empress needed someone equally lovely to distract Gao Zong from the Pure Concubine.

On the first anniversary of his father's death, Gao Zong went to Wu's convent. He carried out his duty of making sacrifices to his father's spirit. Once more, Wu placed herself in his path. She said nothing—she merely gazed at him and began to weep. He too began to cry.

Hearing of this, the empress asked Gao Zong to bring Wu back to the palace. The empress imagined that she could bend Wu to her will. However, Wu was already a master of court intrigue. Within two years, she became closer to Gao Zong than anyone else.

When Wu gave birth to Gao Zong's daughter, the empress came to see her. After she left, Wu smothered the baby. Her servants accused the empress of the evil deed. Wu told Gao Zong that both his wife and the Pure Concubine were plotting against him. He ordered them confined in a secluded part of the palace.

With grand ceremony, Gao Zong proclaimed Wu as the new empress. But she knew that the emperor was weak and liable to change his mind at any time. A person who was disgraced today might return to power tomorrow. Secretly, Wu sent servants to eliminate both of her rivals.

According to the Chinese histories, the servants beat the two women with a hundred blows, cut off their hands and feet, and threw them into a vat of beer. The Pure Concubine, a good Buddhist, believed that her soul would not die, but be reborn into another body. Before dying, she prayed that she would return in the body of a cat, and Wu be reborn as a mouse. "And then," the Pure Concubine vowed, "from life to life I shall tear out her throat." Hearing that, Wu promptly ordered that no cats ever be allowed in the palace.

Flying in the face of tradition, Wu accompanied her husband to meetings with the court officials. Seated behind a screen next to his throne, she listened to the petitions that were read to him. She whispered advice. She told him which officials to promote and which ones to send away. When the blood-drenched spirits of the ex-empress and the Pure Concubine troubled her dreams, she persuaded Gao Zong to move his court to Luoyang, the old Han capital now known as the Eastern Capital.

Some court officials warned the emperor against Wu's grow-

ing influence. But Wu soon demonstrated that she was far more able than her husband. The orders she gave through her husband helped the empire to prosper. As a later Chinese historian wrote, "The Son of Heaven sat on his throne with folded hands, and that was all. Court and country called them the Two Holy Ones."

Wu ruled through a combination of fear and wisdom. She appointed two officials named Lai and Chou to set up a secret police force. They installed their spies everywhere, even within the court. Lai and Chou uncovered countless plots, some real and some imaginary. In their headquarters, they set up a school to teach officials how to torture people to force them to confess their crimes. To deceive prisoners who were brought here, the headquarters had a sign that read "The Gate of the Beautiful View."

Officials in every town and village were ordered to reward anyone who accused others of disloyalty. As the official Chinese history reads, "Consequently there were informers in all parts of the Empire, and people held their tongues."

Yet Wu also sought out the best and most intelligent officials to advise her. Among these was a famous judge who solved puzzling crimes like a Chinese Sherlock Holmes. Known as Judge Dee, he is the hero of many Chinese mystery stories. From trusted people such as Judge Dee, Wu accepted criticism and even disapproval— up to a point.

She liked to tell a story about her days as a girl in Tai Zong's household. Tai Zong had a wild horse that no one could ride. Wu told the emperor she could control the animal, but asked for three things: an iron whip, a mace, and a dagger. If the horse did not respond to being whipped and beaten with the mace, she said, "I will use the dagger and cut his throat." Tai Zong had understood what she meant, said Wu. So did her officials.

One of the secret police chiefs tried to get rid of Judge Dee by accusing him of treason. When Dee was brought to the Gate of the Beautiful View, he was told that if he admitted his crime, his life would be spared. He promptly signed a confession, but that was only to gain time. In jail, Dee wrote a letter to his son on the inner lining of his coat. He asked the jailer to take the coat to his home, because it was too hot. When the son read the letter, he brought it to the empress. She freed her faithful official.

To gain the support of her people, Wu set up a large bronze

urn outside the Imperial City. The humblest citizen could place a note into this "suggestion box." It had four slots, each for a different purpose. One slot was for criticisms of the government. Another was for complaints of injustice. Anyone who wished to become an official could place his application in the third slot. The fourth was for prophecies.

Wu read all the messages that were placed in the box, and relied on them to tell her what the people were really thinking. Anyone who impressed her by cleverness or strength of character could win her favor. She appointed many people of humble birth to high government posts.

This practice secured officials who remained loyal to her when Gao Zong died in the year 683. Wu's eldest son became the new emperor. Wu, now fifty-eight years old, once more seemed to be pushed into the background. But Wu's son was no more an obstacle to her power than her husband had been. With the help of her officials, she deposed him and named her youngest son emperor. This new emperor had no power. He was not even allowed to sit on the throne beside his mother. Wu now ruled China in everything but name.

Others might have been satisfied with that. Not Wu. She announced that a magical stone had been found in the Lo River. On it were carved the words, "The Holy Mother has come among men to rule with perpetual prosperity"—a most favorable sign from Heaven. The Lo River was declared sacred, and people were forbidden to fish in it.

People saw from this that Wu planned to make herself the official ruler. The idea of a woman ruling China in her own name was quite shocking. Some had served as regents for their young sons or weak husbands. But none had ever taken the title of Emperor. Members of the Li family (Tai Zong's relatives) led a rebellion against Wu. They were joined by the husband of Wu's only daughter, Princess Tai Ping.

Wu dearly loved the princess. Many thought she was Wu's favorite child. But whenever Wu was threatened, she showed no mercy. When her generals swiftly put down the rebellion, Wu ordered the leaders executed by having their heads chopped off. As a favor to her daughter, she spared her husband from the execution block. Instead, he was starved to death in prison.

In the year 690, when Wu was sixty-five, she took the final step. She accepted a petition from her son, the supposed emperor. He urged her to establish a new dynasty, with herself as ruler. The Chinese language has no characters that mean "female ruler." So she took the male title—Son of Heaven.

Wu ruled for fifteen more years. When she was seventy, the court was told that she had grown two new teeth. It was a sign that she was still as young and vigorous as ever. But the wisest of her officials, Judge Dee, died in the year 700. Dee had been one of the few who dared to oppose Wu when she was foolish or cruel. Now, whenever she was faced with a difficult problem, she would exclaim, "Why has Heaven taken away my Old Statesman so soon?"

Two brothers named Chang appeared at the palace, and because they amused Wu, she gave them noble titles. The Chang brothers powdered and painted their faces like women and dressed in gaily colored silks. But Wu demanded that everyone at court call the Changs "the Young Masters."

Wu's children had learned to fear their mother and never opposed her wishes. But her grandchildren were not so cautious. Two of them were overheard criticizing the Chang brothers. Wu ordered them flogged to death. She also exiled a court official who warned her about the Changs. But before leaving, he declared, "These two brats will be the cause of a revolution."

He was right. When Wu was eighty, she fell ill. Only the Changs were allowed to visit her. Fearing their influence, the court officials dragged her eldest son back to the palace. Early in the year 705, the plotters killed the Chang brothers and placed Wu under arrest.

She was too old to resist. Her eldest son took his place as the rightful emperor, but he allowed Wu to live out her days under guard in her own palace. She lived for nearly a year, long enough to see her children begin to quarrel among themselves. Growing up in her shadow, none of them was strong enough to hold power.

Later Chinese historians strongly criticized Empress Wu. Yet none denied that for over half a century, she ruled China with only her strong will and intelligence to protect her. In over 3,000 years of Chinese history, Wu Chao was the only woman to be the Son of Heaven.

C H A P T E R 5

THE VAGABOND AND THE
CANDIDATE—LI BO AND DU FU

Poetry has always been an important part of the Chinese culture. Confucius, it was said, assembled China's earliest collection of poems, *The Book of Songs*. Memorizing and studying this poetry became part of traditional Confucian studies. Every gentleman during the Tang Dynasty tried his skill at producing verse in many different forms. Empress Wu made poetry more important by making the ability to write poetry one of the qualifications for her officials. The Tang era produced the two most beloved poets of China—Li Bo and Du Fu.

The two great poets were a study in contrasts. Li Bo was what we might call a "hippie." Carefree and unattached to an official career, he wandered from place to place. It was said that he wrote poems "as easily as water flows out of a fountain." Li Bo represented the Daoist side of Chinese thought. His poems express his eccentric, joyful spirit. One of them reads,

> Life in the World is but a big dream;
> I will not spoil it by any labor or care.

Du Fu, on the other hand, followed the Confucian ideal. He strove for respectability and fervently wished to serve as an official. His poems express a strong sense of social responsibility. One of them reads:

> A white horse
> comes running
> from the northeast.
> two arrows
> sticking up
> from the empty saddle
> and the rider
> poor devil
> who can tell his story now?

How his commander
was killed, how he fought
wounded, at midnight
so many deaths
have come from this fighting!
I start to cry
my tears won't stop.

The two poets met in 744 during the reign of Empress Wu's grandson, Xuan Zong. Though their personalities were very different, they formed a strong friendship that lasted for life. They lived in an era that saw China's arts rise to glorious heights. However, Xuan Zong's reign was to end in tragedy, in both the personal and national realms. The two great poets shared both the glory and tragedy of their times.

Li Bo was born in 701 in one of the far outposts of the Silk Road in Central Asia. As a boy, he moved to Sichuan, about 100 miles northeast of today's Chengdu. He particularly loved books of strange tales and travel and started writing poetry at an early age.

When Li was about twenty his life took a new turn. He met a hermit known as the Master of the Eastern Cliff. His life of solitude appealed to the young man. Li left his home and family to live in the mountains and commune with nature. This was the beginning of a lifelong interest in meditation and spiritual discipline. "For several years," Li recalled, "I never set foot in any town. I kept thousands of rare birds who came and ate out of my hand when I called them, without any trace of fear and suspicion." The Chinese believed that birds were drawn to people of deep spirituality.

After coming down from the mountain, Li Bo went off on a different tack. Showing the romantic side of his character, he became a *hsieh*. Hsiehs were the Chinese version of Robin Hoods. They roamed about the country, defending the weak and the poor. They sought revenge for women and children who had been wronged by others. Stories of hsiehs date far back into Chinese history. Though they broke the law, people respected them. To many Chinese, getting help from a hsieh was a more honorable way to obtain justice than using the legal system. According to a friend, Li Bo "ran his sword through quite a number of people" during his career as a hsieh.

But once again, Li showed his changeable nature. He abandoned his life of action and returned to meditation. He settled down as a disciple of a great Daoist sage. Throughout the rest of his life, Li would be devoted to Daoism. He acquired the nickname "Banished Immortal," a Daoist term for one who been sent to earth for a while because he had misbehaved in heaven. Such people could be spotted by their unconventional behavior—and that certainly applied to Li Bo!

Li Bo listened to the Daoist teacher until, as he said, his mind ran free through space like a "wind wheel." But when the sage asked his disciples to give up drinking wine, Li moved on. That was too great a sacrifice.

He met and married the first of his four wives. He neglected all four, being ever-ready to run off with other poets whose spirits were as free as his. One group that he joined was known as the "Six Idlers of the Bamboo Grove." Another of his clubs called itself "The Eight Immortals of the Wine Cup." Li wrote a couplet that aptly describes his attitude toward life:

> Forever committed to carefree play,
> We'll all meet again in the Milky Way.

A new stage in Li's career began when his poetry attracted the attention of the emperor Xuan Zong. The emperor summoned him to Changan in 742. The emperor's court included a theater and orchestra, entertainment that was new to Li. The poet tried his hand at playing polo, and basked in the hot baths that the city provided for those who could afford to pay. As a favored poet of the court, Li had plenty of money.

At first, Li amused the emperor with his poems and tales of his colorful exploits. He jokingly claimed kinship with the emperor because they were both of the Li family. (Li was one of the most common names in China.) In his wanderings, Li had picked up a knowledge of many languages, a talent that dazzled the emperor.

However, Li soon wore out his welcome. One day he was sitting in a tavern when a messenger came with a summons to appear at the palace. "Tell the emperor," said Li Bo, "that I'm talking with the gods," and fell asleep on the table. Another time, he came to read a poem while drunk, and threw up all over the emperor's clothing.

Disgraced, Li was sent into exile. It was at this time that he met Du Fu. The two traveled together for a short time. Li wrote a playful poem describing his friend:

On Boiled Rice Mountain
I met Du Fu
wearing a big round
bamboo hat
in the hot noon sun.
Du Fu
how come
you've grown
so thin?
You must be suffering
too much
from poetry!

Du Fu was eleven years younger than Li Bo. He grew up north of the city of Luoyang in a cave reinforced with bricks. His family home can still be seen today. When he was very young, his mother died, and he was raised by an aunt to whom he was devoted. Years later, he looked back fondly on his youth:

I remember in my fifteenth year my heart was still childish:
Strong as a brown calf, I ran to and fro.
When pears and dates ripened in the courtyard in the eighth
     month,
In a single day I could climb the trees a thousand times.

But even as a boy, Du Fu had a more serious side. His father and many ancestors were Confucian scholars. Du grew up with the ambition to become a public official. He began his Confucian studies to prepare for examinations that could qualify him for the emperor's service.

From the time of the Han Dynasty, some imperial officials were chosen through a system of state examinations. To pass, the candidate had to have a complete mastery of the Confucian classics, as well as certain later writings on Confucianism. Over time, more officials were selected through this exam system. By the Tang era, more than half were. Du Fu devoted himself to his studies, for the competition in the exams was fierce. It was one way that even the humblest farm boy could become a great man, bringing honor to his family and village. (The exams were open only to males.)

When Du Fu was about twenty-four years old, he came to Changan to take the examinations. He was a very confident young man, and it was a severe blow when he failed to pass. He wrote a letter in which he seemed to blame himself. It was not unusual to fail, and the vast majority of candidates did. Some took the tests for years, trying again and again. Still, the experience was a bitter one.

He tried to forget his disappointment by traveling in the south. He visited temples and enjoyed the natural beauty of the cliffs, valleys, and mountains. But the news that his father had died brought him home. Du Fu observed the twenty-seven months of mourning that Confucian tradition required. The death of his beloved aunt increased his sense of sorrow and loss.

Depressed and discouraged, Du Fu met a completely different spirit—Li Bo. The carefree older man made a deep impression on him. Later, Du Fu wrote a poem addressed to him:

Three nights in a row
I dreamed of you, old friend
so real I could have touched you!
You left in a hurry...
Leaving, framed in the doorway,
you scratched your snowy head
I knew you didn't want to go
Bureaucrats
fatten the capital
while a poet goes cold and hungry
If there is justice in heaven
what sent you out
to banishment?
Ages to come
will warm themselves
at your verses.

Although Du Fu loved his friend, he was not tempted to follow his way of life. He went back to Changan and resumed his efforts to become an official. By now he had a wife and children, and needed to support them. A special examination was scheduled for those who "possessed a special art." As a noted poet, Du Fu was eligible. But no one passed. He expressed his feelings in a poem:

I suddenly thought to "seek to stretch myself."
But in the blue sky my wings drooped;
Checked, I could not swim freely.

Du Fu tried to find a rich patron to support himself and his family. He picked up crumbs, but success eluded him. He felt bitter and frustrated. Du Fu realized that his ambition was a monster. He saw men with lesser talents prospering, and he could not give up his hopes for success. He often talked of leaving Changan, but the charms of the capital kept him there. However, his failure gave him a deeper sense of the sufferings of others. Soon, the whole nation would once again be plunged into disorder, and both Du Fu and Li Bo would be caught up in the events of their time.

The court of the Tang emperor had reached the height of the dynasty's cultural splendor. Xuan Zong's artists and musicians produced great music, painting, and literature. But the Son of Heaven had fallen in love. His beloved was Lady Yang Guifei, the most famous beauty in Chinese history. Messengers on horseback traveled around the clock to provide the Lady Yang's favorite litchi nuts from the south. The emperor was so infatuated with her that he began to neglect his duties. And China faced important threats.

The first sign of trouble came with the defeat of Chinese troops in Central Asia in 751. Natural disasters followed, bringing the ominous signs that Heaven was displeased with the emperor. Seasons of never-ending rain caused mudslides that destroyed villages. Crops were washed away, and poverty stalked the countryside. For Du Fu, poverty caused personal tragedy. He had sent his family to a town north of the capital. In the year 754, illness took the life of his infant son. He wrote bitter verses contrasting the emperor's lavish court with the life of ordinary people:

> Women like goddesses
> are dancing inside
> all silk and perfume
> guests in sable furs
> music of pipes and fiddles
> camel-pad broth being served
> with frosted oranges and pungent tangerines.
> Behind those red gates
> meat and wine are left to spoil
> outside lie the bones
> of people who starved and froze
> luxury and misery a few feet apart!
> My heart aches to think about it.

The emperor's devotion to the Lady Yang brought about his downfall. At Lady Yang's urging, he appointed an ambitious, grossly fat Turkish soldier named An Lushan to command the forces along the northern border. At the end of the year 755, An Lushan raised the banner of rebellion, trying to make himself emperor. He moved south and captured Changan.

Xuan Zong fled, taking Lady Yang with him. But on the outskirts of the city, his soldiers revolted. They blamed Lady Yang for the disorder and would not proceed until she was dead. She was strangled with a silk handkerchief. The emperor fled to Sichuan, where he abdicated in favor of his son. After eight years of warfare, the Tang army recovered Changan and put down the rebellion. The Tang Dynasty continued for another 150 years, but never with the same confidence and glory.

These momentous events affected the lives of the two great poets. Li Bo became involved in the intrigue that followed the rebellion. He backed a member of the imperial family who lost out in the struggle for the throne. Li Bo was fortunate not to be executed. He was imprisoned for a time and then banished to a distant region. He spent his remaining years wandering, writing, and drinking. His poems took on a new tone, reflecting the bloodshed and fighting that he had seen:

> Hand to hand, swords flashing
> men grapple and die in the field
> horses fall, their squeals
> drift skyward
> the crows and kites

peck for human guts
carry them off in their beaks
and hang them on dead trees.
What have the generals accomplished?
What they know
is less than what we've learned—
a sword's a stinking thing
a wise man will use
as seldom as he can.

Li Bo died in the year 762. Supposedly, he was crossing a river in a boat after a night of drinking. Spying the moon's reflection in the water, he leaned over the rail to embrace it. He fell in and was drowned.

Du Fu, on the other hand, was captured by the rebel army and lived in the occupied capital city. He was frantic with worry about his wife and family, who were separated from him. He wrote:

Tonight
in this same moonlight
my wife is alone at her window
her hair must be damp from the mist
her arms cold jade in the moonlight
when will we stand together
by those slack curtains
while the moonlight
dries the tear-streaks
on our faces?

After the Tang forces retook the city, Du Fu obtained the government post he had sought for so long. He was named an Omissioner of the Left. It was his duty to bring to the court's attention matters that had been neglected, or "omitted." Now, however, the office was an empty prize. He soon resigned and left Changan, never to return.

Du Fu built himself a thatched hut in Chengdu, where he led a simple life. He continued to travel, writing poems about the fighting that still engulfed the countryside. Like his friend Li Bo, he died of drowning, when his boat overturned.

Neither Li Bo nor Du Fu knew that in the centuries to come, countless candidates for the imperial examinations would have to memorize their poems to pass. To Li Bo, the happy vagabond, it might have seemed a great joke. Du Fu, the frustrated candidate at those same examinations, might have found it a bitter triumph.

CHAPTER 6

ONE-CORNER MA—MA YUAN

Painting was a passion at the imperial court during the Song Dynasty. The Emperor Hui Zong was himself a skilled painter, specializing in birds and flowers. He gathered talented artists at an Academy of Painting at the Song capital, Kaifeng, on the Huang He River. The palace even had a special artist on call at night to paint any incident regarded as worthy of royal attention. All government officials had to display an ability to paint in addition to skill at calligraphy and composing poems.

Hui Zong's generosity to his court painters brought many applicants for the posts. The emperor instituted palace examinations to select the best artists. Candidates were required to illustrate a passage from Chinese poetry. Hui Zong provided the following couplet as a model:

> When I return from trampling flowers,
> the hoofs of my horse are fragrant.

The painting that was judged best tells us much about Chinese art. Did you think that the picture would show horses running through flowered fields? Not so. In the winning painting, a horse is walking along a track with butterflies flying around his heels. No fields or flowers were to be seen. Instead, the fluttering butterflies imply the fragrance and show the time is spring. In Chinese art, pictures often suggest things rather than show them directly. Imagination in portraying a subject is highly valued. The viewer is invited to share the creative process with the painter.

Unfortunately, Hui Zong was not as good at ruling as he was at painting. A fierce tribe called the Nuzhen attacked China from the north in 1126 and sacked the capital. The emperor was carried off to Manchuria, where he died after nine years in captivity.

However, a relative escaped, taking much of the imperial art collection and painters with him. He set up a new court at Hangzhou, south of the Yangzi River. From Hangzhou, the

Southern Song Dynasty ruled a smaller Chinese empire, but one that still included sixty million citizens. Among the court painters of the new emperor were the grandfather and father of Ma Yuan.

Ma Yuan was born sometime around the middle of the twelfth century. He represented the fourth generation of a renowned family of painters. The earliest member, Ma Fen, became famous for his images of Buddhist saints. He also specialized in scenes of wildlife, birds, and flowers.

His son Ma Xing, Ma Yuan's grandfather, was a favorite painter of Hui Zong, who consulted him on the selection of art works for the imperial collection. Ma Xing played a similar role for the new emperor at Hangzhou. The personal friendship between Ma Xing and the emperor strengthened after Xing painted a lovely portrait of the ruler's favorite concubine. Xing was able to have his son appointed as a court painter.

Thus, Ma Yuan and his older brother both grew up at the splendid court of the Southern Song. Inevitably, both of them would follow the family tradition of painting, although Ma Yuan's talent would be far greater.

By the age of five, young Ma was using his brush. In China the same instrument is used for both writing and painting. By tradition, Meng Tian, the Qin general who directed the building of the Great Wall, is credited with developing the writing brush. In China the art of writing, or calligraphy, is highly respected. Chinese believe that a person's handwriting is the mirror of his character. Each symbol of the written language is a form of abstract art. "Every horizontal stroke," wrote a famous calligrapher, "is like a mass of clouds in battle formation. Every hook like a bent bow of the greatest strength. Every dot like a fallen rock from a high peak."

The Chinese called the instruments of writing the Four Treasures. Paper, brush, inkstone, and ink were used to create writing, poetry, and painting. In China these three arts are related. The effect of a poem came not just from the words but also from the way the characters looked on the paper. In painting, the quality of the brushstrokes was the most important element. The brushstrokes were said to be the "heartbeat" of the painter. Often, paintings also included a poem, and its calligraphy was as important as the subject matter of the painting.

Young Ma practiced constantly to develop a handsome calligraphy. Each character requires several strokes (as many as fifty for a single character), and these had to be made in a specific order. There was no way to erase. So before Ma wrote a character, he had to memorize the sequence of strokes. It was good preparation for his painting.

Chinese painters did not use oil paints, which allow artists to paint over their mistakes or correct false starts. The Chinese artist, putting his water-based paint on silk or paper, cannot change his mind after beginning the work. The brush strokes must be made lightly and rapidly so they do not spread.

"Grasp the brush," wrote a Song painter, "Look intently [at the paper], then visualize what you are going to paint. Follow your vision quickly, lift your brush and pursue directly that which you see, as a falcon dives on the springing hare—the least slackening and it will escape you."

Ma's efforts paid off. He took the competitive examinations for the Academy of Painting and passed. He was accepted as a student, the lowest order of membership. He received a small salary and the opportunity to pursue his chosen career.

The Painting Academy, where he now lived, was in a beautiful section of Hangzhou. It was dominated by the Lingyin Temple, a Buddhist monastery. To the west, Ma could see Lingyin Mountain, with its strangely shaped rocks resembling plants and animals. On the other side was Hangzhou's West Lake, which was part of the imperial residence.

Life was sweet for Ma. Hangzhou provided more luxuries for the privileged than any other city in the world at the time. He ate off lacquer dishes and drank tea from porcelain cups. West Lake was a source of fresh water for the city, and the standard of hygiene was high. Ma took hot baths with perfumed liquid soap and used toilet paper—unknown anywhere else in the world.

Along the Imperial Way, Hangzhou's main street, vendors hawked a dazzling variety of wares. Some set up portable stoves to cook noodles and other "fast foods." Chefs prepared more elaborate meals to be delivered to homes of wealthy citizens. The Chinese loved to display fresh flowers in their homes, and many delicate and rare types were available. By this time, the Chinese had developed printing, and Ma could browse in the city's bookstores and pay for his purchases with paper money, another Chinese invention.

Rivers and streams ran through Hangzhou, and people crossed arched stone bridges to go from one part of the city to another. Acrobats, musicians, and storytellers performed near the bridges in return for coins from the crowds. The frequent festival days brought colorful parades and fireworks into the streets.

Women wore white makeup on their faces and rouged their cheeks. Their fingernails were polished bright pink. The women walked with a mincing gait because the cruel custom of foot-binding had caught on. To achieve the tiny "golden lilies," young girls suffered the pains of tight bandages that actually stunted the growth of their feet.

As Ma's painting skills developed, he passed other examinations to achieve the rank of Scholar of Art and then Painter-in-Waiting. Now he was allowed to wear scarlet robes with a fish-shaped badge of gold and jade. Finally, Emperor Ning Zong, a great lover of painting, conferred the highest honors on Ma Yuan. He received the Golden Belt and the title Painter-in-Attendance, just as his father and grandfather had. Ma moved to the imperial palace grounds and shared the prestige and privileges of the highest officials.

Several of Ma's paintings survive in museums, including a portrait of Confucius. Because no images of Confucius were made during his lifetime, Ma was free to use his imagination. He painted a dignified figure in a long robe with wide sleeves that hide his hands. To show the spirit of Confucius as a sage, Ma enlarged the height and size of his forehead and gave him a gentle smile.

However, Ma Yuan's most famous paintings are his landscapes. Artists of the Song era were particularly skilled at this form of art. Of all forms of Chinese art, landscapes are the most popular, reflecting a deep love of nature. Daoists believe that the peaks of certain mountains are the homes of the immortals. The Chinese word for "landscape" is *shan-shuei*, which means "mountains-water."

"It is human nature," wrote a landscape master of the Song Dynasty,

> to resent the hustle and bustle of society, and to wish to see, but not always succeed in seeing, immortals hidden in the clouds.

51

We are usually excluded from the sights and sounds of Nature. Now the artist has reproduced it for us. One can imagine oneself sitting on the rocks in a gully and hearing the cries of monkeys and birds; while in one's own sitting-room the light of the mountains and the colors of the water dazzle one's eyes. Is it not a joy, a fulfillment of one's dream? That is why paintings of landscapes are so much in demand.

During the Northern Song Dynasty, painters had depicted the rugged mountains of the north. Around the southern capital, nature showed a gentler aspect. Ma became famous for his views of the area, using muted colors or black and gray ink. In *Angler on a Wintry Lake*, he portrayed a fisherman on the West Lake. The painting includes the first known picture of a fishing reel, a Chinese invention.

Ma loved pine trees and painted them as simple, elegant spires. He was also fond of gnarled and crooked trees that had endured years of wind and rain. His paintings of stunted trees became so famous that they started a new fashion in gardening. People tried to imitate Ma's models by tying and trimming the limbs of young trees, growing them into grotesque shapes that were called "ma yuans."

Ma also produced handscroll landscapes. A handscroll, or long, rolled-up sheet of paper, could be examined at leisure, pro-

longing the enjoyment of the experience. A viewer unrolled the scroll from right to left and looked at portions only as large as was convenient. Chinese collectors delighted in sharing with friends the enjoyment of viewing these treasures.

Some handscrolls depicted historical incidents. Ma's *Four Sages of Shang Shan* is based on a story of four wise men who lived around 200 B.C. The era was a time of civil war, and four wise men withdrew from the world to escape the strife. Water, rocks, and pine trees dwarf the figures wandering through the scroll. The story is retold in calligraphy painted against the sky. (It is said that the wife of the emperor was so fond of Ma's paintings that she personally painted the calligraphy on some of them. It was a great honor for the painter.)

As Ma grew older, he developed a unique style. He began to concentrate the subject matter of his paintings into a smaller and smaller part of the paper. An example is *A Scholar and his Servant on the Terrace*, painted on silk in black ink and light colors. At the lower corner of the paper, a small human figure stands looking into a vast landscape. The tree in the foreground is sharply drawn. Just beyond the scholar are suggestions of trees seen through the mist. More than half the paper is blank. The emptiness suggests a limitless space with an eerie, spiritual quality.

Such paintings gave the artist the nickname "One-corner Ma." The description referred not only to his style, but also to the teaching of Confucius. As you read in Chapter 1, Confucius told his students that if he gave them one corner of an idea, he expected them to come back with the other three. This idea applied equally to thinking and painting. The viewer's imagination filled in the three corners of the paintings that Ma left blank.

Ma led a long, productive life. He nurtured the career of his son, Ma Lin, who became the last of the Ma family to serve at the emperor's court. It is said that Ma Yuan allowed his son to sign some of the work that the master himself had completed. This helped the young man get a good start on his own career.

Ma Yuan's paintings influenced Chinese art for centuries. They became popular in the neighboring nations of Japan and Korea, and painters there adopted him as a model. Even today, art lovers study with pleasure the works that survive in museums. Ma Yuan is admired as one of the great artists in world history.

CHAPTER 7

THE ADMIRAL OF THE WESTERN SEAS—ZHENG HE

In the 1930s, a stone pillar was discovered in a town in Fujian province. It held an inscription that described the amazing voyages of a Chinese admiral named Zheng He. Five hundred years earlier, Zheng He had chosen "a lucky day" to place this pillar in the Temple of the Celestial Spouse, a Daoist goddess.

Zheng He described how the emperor of the Ming Dynasty had ordered him to sail to "the countries beyond the horizon," all the way to "the end of the earth." His mission was to display the might of Chinese power and collect tribute from the "barbarians from beyond the seas."

The pillar contains the Chinese names for the countries Zheng He visited. Altogether, Zheng He visited thirty nations from Asia to Africa, traveling more than "one hundred thousand li," about 35,000 miles. He wrote:

> We have...beheld in the ocean huge waves like mountains rising sky-high, and we have set eyes on barbarian regions far away hidden in a blue transparency of light vapors, while our sails, loftily unfurled like clouds, day and night continued their course, rapid like that of a star, traversing the savage waves as if we were treading a public thoroughfare.

In all, Zheng He made seven wondrous voyages of discovery between 1405 and 1433. His achievements show that China had the ships and navigational skills to explore the world. Mysteriously, China did not follow up on these voyages. The Chinese destroyed their ocean-going ships and halted further expeditions. Thus, a century later, Europeans would "discover" China, instead of the Chinese "discovering" Europe.

China has a very old seafaring tradition. Chinese ships had sailed to India as early as the Han Dynasty. Chinese sailors had an important invention to help them—the compass. The compass, or

"south-pointing spoon," started out as a fortune-telling instrument used like a Ouija board. By the Song era, sailors had taken it up. As a foreign ship captain wrote, "In dark weather they look to the south-pointing needle, and use a sounding line to determine the smell and nature of the mud on the sea bottom, and so know where they are."

Chinese shipbuilders also developed fore-and-aft sails, the stern post rudder, and boats with paddlewheels. Watertight compartments below decks kept the ship from sinking. Some boats were armor plated for protection. All these developments made long-distance navigation possible.

After the Mongols were overthrown in 1368, the emperor of the new Ming ("bright") Dynasty wanted to assert Chinese power. Because China was no longer part of a land empire that stretched from Asia to Europe, the emperor turned to the sea. He decided to build a navy. The Chinese made elaborate plans that would not be fulfilled for many years. A shipyard was built at the new capital of Nanjing. Thousands of varnish and tung trees were planted on nearby Purple Mountain to provide wood for shipbuilding. The emperor established a school of foreign languages to train interpreters. While all this was going on, the man who would lead the navy was still an infant.

Zheng He was born in 1371 in Kunyang, a town in southwest Yunnan Province. His family, named Ma, were part of a minority group known as the Semur. They originally came from Central Asia and followed the religion of Islam. Both his grandfather and father had made the Muslim pilgrimage to Mecca. Zheng He grew up hearing their accounts of travel through foreign lands.

Yunnan was one of the last strongholds of Mongol support, holding out long after the Ming Dynasty began. After Ming armies conquered Yunnan in 1382, Zheng He was taken captive and brought to Nanjing. The eleven-year-old boy was made a servant of the prince who would become the Yongle Emperor. (Yongle means "Perpetual Happiness.") It was Yongle who renamed the boy Zheng He.

Zheng is described in Chinese historical records as tall and heavy, with "clear-cut features and long ear lobes; a stride like a tiger's and a voice clear and vibrant." Zheng was well liked and admired for his quick wit in argument. Moreover, he was a brave soldier. When his prince seized the Chinese throne from his nephew, Zheng He fought well on his behalf. As a result, Zheng He became a close confidant of the new emperor and was given an important position at court.

The Yongle Emperor had ambitious plans. A vigorous man, he rebuilt the Great Wall to the condition in which it exists today. He also built his new capital at Beijing, next to the remains of the former Yuan capital. The emperor decided to go ahead with the sea voyages that had long been planned. He appointed Zheng He to lead them and gave him the title "Admiral of the Western Seas."

At each country Zheng He visited, he was to present gifts from the emperor and to exact tribute for the glory of the Ming. The Chinese had a unique view of foreign relations. Because China developed its culture in isolation from other great civilizations, it saw itself as the center of the world. The Chinese called their country "the Middle Kingdom."

The Chinese emperor's duty was to attract "all under heaven" to be civilized in Confucian harmony. When foreign ambassadors came to the Chinese court, they "kowtowed" as they approached the emperor. (The required process of "kowtow" was to kneel three times and bow one's head to the floor three times at each kneeling.) In return for tribute from other countries, the emperor sent gifts and special seals that confirmed their rulers' authority. In fact, these foreign kings were officially made part of the Ming Dynasty.

In 1405 Zheng He set out on his first voyage. No nation on earth had ever sent such a fleet onto the ocean. It included sixty-two large ships, some 600 feet long, larger than any others on the seas. Hundreds of smaller vessels accompanied them. A Chinese historian described them, "The ships which sail the Southern Sea are like houses. When their sails are spread they are like great clouds in the sky."

Zheng He's first port of call was in Champa, a part of today's Vietnam. He was surprised to find many Chinese living there. Merchants and craftsmen had emigrated from the coastal provinces since the time of the Tang Dynasty. They had already helped to spread Confucian ideals, and Champa's ruler willingly offered tribute for the Chinese emperor. In return, of course, Zheng He presented the king with lavish gifts that were probably more valuable.

Zheng He sailed away from the coast, westward across the Indian Ocean. The ships traveled for days out of sight of any land. Then they encountered a hurricane. The ships tossed wildly in the fierce storm and seemed to be on the verge of sinking. The terrified sailors prepared to die; some prayed to the Daoist goddess called the Celestial Spouse. Then a "divine light" suddenly shone at the tips of the masts. "As soon as this miraculous light appeared, the danger was appeased," Zheng He wrote.

The miraculous light that appeared on the mast was probably St. Elmo's fire, static electricity that is a familiar sight to experienced sailors. Because the sailors had prayed to the Daoist goddess, they believed it was her sign of protection. From then on, they followed wherever Zheng He led them. That was why he later placed a pillar of thanksgiving at the Temple of the Celestial Spouse in Fujian province.

When the Chinese sailors reached Calicut, India, their giant ships created a stir. The ruler there presented his visitors with sashes made of gold spun into hair-fine threads and studded with large pearls and precious stones. The Chinese were entertained with music and song. One crew member wrote that the Indians' musical instruments were "made of gourds with strings of red copper wire, and the sound and rhythm were pleasant to the ear."

On the way back to China, the fleet threaded its way through the Straits of Malacca, stopping at the large islands of Sumatra and Java. Zheng He established a base at the Straits that he would use for each of his seven voyages. There are thousands of smaller islands in this vast archipelago, and some were pirates' lairs. The pirates preyed on unwary fishermen and small merchant vessels. Zheng He, showing how the emperor treated those who disrupted harmony, attacked and destroyed a fleet of pirate ships. He captured the leader and brought him back to Beijing for execution.

He also ran into trouble at Borneo, where the king did not show adequate respect for the ambassadors of the Son of Heaven. Zheng He took him captive. The king spent the rest of his days as a prisoner in Beijing.

When Zheng He returned, the emperor was pleased. He sent his admiral on ever-longer voyages. Seven times, Zheng He's ships set sail for unknown lands. On and on he went, following his orders to travel as far as he could. He reached Arabia, where he fulfilled a personal dream. He made the pilgrimage to Mecca that is the duty of every good Muslim once in his lifetime. He also visited Muhammad's tomb in Medina. On the fifth voyage, he reached the coast of Africa, landing in Somalia on the east coast.

Zheng He organized each expedition on an enormous scale. Some consisted of as many as 27,000 men. Besides sailors and navigators, they included doctors, scribes, shipwrights, and cooks. On some voyages Muslim religious leaders and Buddhist monks were brought along to serve as diplomats in lands where people were Muslim or Buddhist.

Each ship brought enough food to last the whole voyage, in case "barbarian" food was not acceptable. In addition to rice and other food that could be preserved, the ships carried huge tubs of earth on deck so that vegetables and fruit could be grown.

On each voyage the fleet anchored at the Malacca base, where provisions, tribute, and gifts were stored in warehouses. Zheng He found that foreign kings and princes particularly admired the famous blue-and-white Ming porcelain dishes, vases, and cups. Foreigners still yearned for Chinese silk, for cotton printed with Chinese designs, and for the coarse but long-lasting, brownish yellow cloth known as Nankeen because it was made in Nanking (now Nanjing). The holds of Zheng He's ships were also crammed with gold and silver, iron tools, copper kitchenware, and perfumes.

In exchange for such wares, and as tribute, Zheng He brought back medicinal herbs, dyes, spices, precious gems, pearls, rhinoceros horns, ivory, and exotic animals. On the homeward voyage, the fleet again stopped at their base to sort out the foreign goods and wait for a favorable wind to return to China.

The expeditions were an important source of information about foreign countries. A crew member described the Nicobar Islands in the Bay of Bengal off the east coast of India:

> Its inhabitants live in the hollows of trees and caves. Both men and women there go about stark naked, like wild beasts, without a stitch of clothing on them. No rice grows there. The people subsist solely on wild yams, jack fruit, and plantains, or upon the fish which they catch. There is a legend current among them that, if they wear the smallest scrap of clothing, their bodies would break out into sores and ulcers, owing to their ancestors having been cursed by Buddha for having stolen and hidden his clothes while he was bathing.

In Sri Lanka, the Chinese visited Buddhist Temple Hill, where Buddha was said to have left his footprint on a rock. They marveled at all the temples, particularly one that held a relic of the Buddha's tooth. According to a crew member, the people of the island

> do not venture to eat cow's flesh, they merely drink the milk. When a cow dies they bury it. It is capital punishment for anyone to secretly kill a cow; he who does so can however escape punishment by paying a ransom of a cow's head made of solid gold.

Sri Lanka seemed like a treasure island, where rubies and other precious stones were abundant. The people harvested pearls from the sea and had discovered the trick of making cultured pearls by planting a speck of sand inside an oyster's shell.

The king of Sri Lanka was an ardent Buddhist who treated both cows and elephants with religious respect. However, because he did not show proper respect for the ambassadors from the Son of Heaven, he was taken back to China for "instruction." He was returned to his island on a later voyage.

When the Chinese reached the east coast of Africa, they found people who built houses of brick. "Men and women wear their hair in rolls; when they go out they wear a linen hood. There are deep wells worked by means of cog wheels. Fish are caught in the sea with nets." The Africans offered such goods as "dragon saliva, incense, and golden amber." The Chinese found the African animals even more amazing. These included "lions, gold-spotted leopards, and camel-birds [ostriches], which are six or seven feet tall." The most exciting thing that Zheng He ever brought back to the emperor's court was a giraffe.

The animal came from today's Somalia. In the Somali language, the name for giraffe sounds similar to the Chinese word for unicorn. It was easy to imagine that this was the legendary animal that had played an important part in the birth of Confucius. Surely, it must be a sign of Heaven's favor on the emperor's reign.

When the giraffe arrived in 1415, the emperor himself went to the palace gate to receive it, as well as a "celestial horse" (zebra) and a "celestial stag" (oryx). The palace officials offered congratulations and performed the kowtow before the heavenly animals.

When Zheng He came back from his seventh voyage in 1433, he was sixty-two years old. He had accomplished much for China, spreading the glory of the Middle Kingdom to many countries that now sent tribute and ambassadors to the court. Though he died soon afterward, his exploits had won him fame. Plays and novels were written about his voyages. In such places as Malacca and Java, towns, caves, and temples were named after him.

However, a new Ming emperor had come to the throne. His scholar-officials criticized Zheng's achievements, complaining about their great expense. China was now fighting another barbarian enemy on its western borders and needed to devote its resources to that struggle. When a court favorite wanted to continue Zheng He's voyages, he was turned down. To make sure, the court officials destroyed the logs that Zheng He had kept. We know about his voyages only from the pillar and some accounts that his crew members wrote.

Thus, China abandoned its overseas voyages. It was a fateful decision, for just at that time, Portugal was beginning to send its ships down the west coast of Africa. In the centuries that followed, European explorers would sail to all parts of the world. They would establish colonies in Africa, America, and finally in the nations of East Asia. China would suffer because it had turned its back on exploration. Zheng He had started the process that might have led the Middle Kingdom to greater glory. Unfortunately, the rulers of the Ming Dynasty refused to follow his lead.

CHAPTER 8

THE POETIC GOURMET— YUAN MEI

"Cooking is like matrimony," wrote Yuan Mei.

Two things served together should match. I have known people to mix grated lobster with bird's nest, and mint with chicken or pork! The cooks of today think nothing of mixing in one soup the meat of chicken, duck, pig, and goose. But these [animals] doubtless have souls. And these souls will most certainly file complaints in the next world on the way they have been treated in this.

From ancient times, the Chinese have had a love affair with food. It is said that the Chinese not only eat to live but live to eat. A Chinese guest is more likely to inquire about the health of the family cook than to make small talk about the weather. The pleasure of a fine meal begins when the guests learn what is to be served and is prolonged by discussing its delights after it is eaten. Chinese scholars such as Yuan Mei—and Confucius himself—have always regarded food as a serious subject. Indeed, some legends claim Confucius spent so much time away from home because his wife would not prepare his food the way he wanted it.

Each kind of food also required a different kind of presentation at the table. An American Thanksgiving turkey dinner, brought to the table as a complete roasted bird, would be regarded as "barbaric." Cutting up the food was a job for the cooks—before they served it.

Because the meal was served in bite-sized pieces, the Chinese used chopsticks to eat it. Small children learned how to pick up food morsels by pinching together the two sticks made of wood, bone, or ivory. The Chinese word for "chopsticks" is *kwai-tsze*, meaning "quick ones."

Over the centuries, the Chinese have eaten a great variety of foods. However, the definition of what makes up a proper Chinese meal has remained constant. It must have two elements: grains, usually rice, and other starch foods (called *fan*) and vegetable or meat dishes (*ts'ai*). To be both satisfying and healthy, meals must blend these foods in the proper proportions.

The Chinese saw a connection between proper food and good health. Chinese nutrition was bound up with the ancient idea of *yin* and *yang*. These are the positive and negative forces in the universe. Some have likened them to the universe breathing in and breathing out. Yin is feminine and dark. Yang is masculine and bright. But neither is superior to the other—both are required to be in balance for harmony. You have probably seen the yin-yang symbol, a circle divided by a wavy line into black and white halves. It represents an idea of dual forces in the universe that Chinese believed in even before the time of Confucius.

Each type of food has its yin or yang value, and a skilled cook knows how to balance them for a healthy meal. Illness or pain show that the body is out of balance. Doctors advise their patients to eat more of a certain kind of food to correct the imbalance.

Yuan Mei was the foremost writer of his day. A sociable fellow, his favorite subject of conversation was food. His book *Shih Tan* ("The Menu") is a collection of recipes and thoughts on food that he accumulated over a lifetime. He sent his cook to find out how to make new dishes that he had enjoyed or heard about. Food was more than a hobby with him. He felt that the art of preparing a meal was a moral virtue.

Yuan Mei was born in Hangzhou in 1716. His family was poor, and Yuan was raised by his kindly Aunt Shen. As he later recalled, "when I was cold, [Aunt Shen] wrapped me up, scratched my back when it itched, washed my face in the morning, and gave me my bath at night." His aunt was a great storyteller and entertained him with tales about China's ancient supernatural heroes.

Everyone saw that Yuan Mei was a bright child, and a neighbor even offered to be his teacher. Yuan loved poetry and books. "Books," he wrote, "became to me dearer than life itself." At the age of eleven, Yuan passed the local Boys' Test, which made him eligible for the examination ordeal that was the main road to success in the Chinese empire. When he passed his First Degree exam, he became a National Student and was permitted to wear a silver

badge on his cap to indicate that he had reached this goal.

Now Yuan Mei had to practice writing the "eight-legged essay." This was the precise form required for examination answers above the First Degree. It got its name because it required eight separate paragraphs. Each paragraph had to develop a specific aspect of the topic. The poem forms were equally rigid. Test-takers had to memorize rhyme-tables that showed, among other things, how a particular word was pronounced over a thousand years earlier. Just like the students who take college entrance exams today, Yuan bought cram-books that told him how to pass.

When Yuan took the Second Degree test, he went to a building with several thousand small rooms, just large enough for one test-taker, a chair, and a table. Yuan, like everybody else, was locked within one of these cells for three days to complete the first part of the test. Guards checked that servants bringing food and water did not smuggle in books. Even so, some candidates used elaborate ways to cheat, such as writing out long texts in tiny characters on the inside of their jacket lining. After the first part was over, the candidates had a day of rest. Then the routine was repeated two more times. Each completed test was identified only by a number so that the judges could not favor students that they knew.

Ambitious students came from all over China to take the Third Degree test at the imperial capital, Beijing. Those who failed returned to their villages to study and try again. Many continued to take the tests for years; a few spent their entire lifetimes doing so. Sometimes the emperor granted honorary degrees to aged men who had never passed. But Yuan passed on his first try.

He was accepted at the Hanlin Academy, which had been founded during the Tang Dynasty over a thousand years earlier. This was a particular honor, bestowed on those who had finished highest in the Third Degree tests. The academy's spirit was free and open. Older scholars welcomed the younger ones, and all shared the delights of studying and discussing literature, arts, and philosophy. Members of the academy were often assigned to court duty.

Yuan was excited to be working at the imperial court, though thousands of people worked there, and he seldom saw the emperor. Yuan gained a chance for further advancement by being assigned to study the culture of the Manchus, who had overthrown the Ming rulers and taken control of China less than a century before.

The last years of the Ming Dynasty had been marked by rebellion and a series of inept emperors. In 1644 the Manchus, a people from the northeast, had taken advantage of the confusion to sweep down and capture Beijing. They proclaimed a new dynasty. The Manchu, or Qing, was the second foreign dynasty to rule China. But the Manchu emperors adopted Chinese ceremonies and sponsored Confucian learning with the same fervor as other emperors. Confucianism appealed to them because of its stress on order and respect for authority. As the new authority, they wanted their subjects to obey them.

However, the Manchus put their own stamp on Chinese society. They issued an order requiring all Chinese men to shave their foreheads and wear their hair in a queue, or braid. The common saying for this was, "Lose your hair and keep your head, or keep your hair and lose your head." The Manchus also imposed their style of dress. Men had to wear a tight, high-collared jacket buttoned at the right shoulder, instead of the loose robes common in earlier times.

Unfortunately for Yuan Mei, he scored last in his class on the test in Manchu culture. As a result, he was assigned to an unimportant post in the provinces. He eventually became a magistrate in a district of the city of Nanjing. A magistrate was responsible for taxation, law, and the welfare of his district. People came to his *yamen*, or official headquarters, with their complaints. The magistrate was both judge and jury in all legal matters.

Yuan Mei became well known for his wise decisions. Two families in his district had been quarreling for many years over the ownership of a field. When Yuan arrived, both sides appeared with stacks of old documents proving their right to the land. Yuan studied the pile of papers and said, "If things go on like this, you will both be ruined. Let me wind up the case for you." He pushed the papers aside and drew a line down a map of the field. Each family received one part of the field.

As a magistrate, Yuan Mei frequently had to entertain guests. He hired a cook, named Wang, who introduced Yuan to the joy of eating well. When Wang first came to the household, Yuan "feared he had grand ideas, and I explained to him that I came from a family that was far from rich and that we were not in the habit of spending a fortune on every meal."

Chef Wang laughed and soon brought out a bowl of plain vegetable soup, "which was so good," wrote Yuan, "that one went on and on taking it till one really felt one needed nothing more." Yuan Mei was hooked. From then on, he let Wang prepare anything he liked.

Wang was a tyrant in his kitchen. He insisted on doing all the shopping himself, rather than sending a servant. He told Yuan, "I must see things in their natural state before I can decide whether I can apply my art to them." He refused to make more than six or seven dishes for a meal, even when his master asked for more.

Yuan was amazed at the delicious meals his cook could make out of the simplest ingredients. Chef Wang told him, "if one has the art, then a piece of celery or salted cabbage can be made into a marvelous delicacy." But if a cook had no artistry, it didn't matter if he used "the greatest delicacies and rarities of land, sea, or sky."

The relationship between the two men was sometimes stormy. As the years passed, Yuan Mei grew bold enough to criticize some dishes. The temperamental Chef Wang said, "You...continually criticize me, abuse me, fly into a rage with me, but on such an occasion, make me aware of some real defect; so that I would a thousand times rather listen to your bitter admonitions than to the sweetest praise....Say no more! I mean to stay on here." After the chef died, Yuan Mei said, "Now I never sit down to a meal without thinking of him and shedding a tear."

After a short official career, Yuan did the unthinkable: he resigned his post. He complained that he didn't like all the ceremony of dealing with superiors, "which I am very bad at." Yuan believed this got in the way of his real job—helping ordinary people, "which I do very well."

Yuan retired to his home in Nanjing to tend his garden, write poetry, and collect recipes for a book he planned to write on cooking. In his garden, he created a miniature model of the famous West Lake in his native Hangzhou. It offered the same kind of enjoyment as a landscape painting. "If I were still living at Hangzhou," he wrote, "I could not spend all day and every day at the Lake. But here I can live at home and yet live beside the Lake."

He began to write poetry and stories of supernatural events. He had always admired strange tales and now created his own. He told of a scholar who was visited in the night by green monsters

and dwarfs. In another tale, a marriage broker arranges a wedding between two ghosts who have haunted their former spouses. Yuan shared these tales with a friend who was famous for his paintings of ghosts.

Yuan enjoyed inviting groups of close friends to share a meal and good conversation. He was a witty, affectionate, and generous friend, especially to young poets who sought advice. Soon he had a regular circle that gathered at his home—virtually a school. When he accepted women among his students, other friends strongly criticized him. For scholarship in China was almost exclusively a male domain. No women were allowed to take the imperial exams. But Yuan welcomed his students on the basis of their intelligence and talents, and he saw these were not restricted to men. He also advocated a ban on footbinding.

Wealthy people liked to invite Yuan to their homes, both to enjoy his witty conversation and to see if he would approve of their chefs' cooking. The cooking style of the Qing Dynasty was typically lavish. One typical banquet included more than 30 separate dishes with such names as: "Deer Heart Garnished With Plums," "Dragon Liver and Phoenix Marrow" [chicken liver and brains], "Sparrow's Tongues," "Bear's Paw and Partridge," and "Sauteed Shark's Fins."

But Yuan often surprised his hosts by criticizing their vulgar display of elaborate, costly, and rare foods. Yuan Mei did not enjoy such fancy dishes as much as well-cooked, simple food. In his cookbook, Yuan Mei has two basic rules: "Don't eat with your ears. Don't eat with your eyes." The first rule meant not to serve unusual foods just so your guests will comment on them. According to Yuan, bird's-nest soup, a Chinese delicacy, was not as tasty as good common bean curd. The second rule meant not to cover the table with innumerable dishes and courses to dazzle your guests. "For this is to eat with the eyes, not with the mouth."

Writing the cookbook was a labor of love that lasted nearly his whole life. He did not publish it until he was past eighty. It contains many stories about his eating experiences. In one, Yuan recalled a man of Beijing who was fond of inviting guests, but served them poor food.

> One day a guest said to him, "Do you count me as a good friend?" "Certainly I do," said the host. The guest then knelt in front of him, saying, "If you are indeed my friend, I have a request to make to you, and I shall not rise from my knees until it is granted." "What is your request?" asked the astonished host. "That you will promise," said the guest, "that in the future when you ask people to dinner, you will not ask me."

In his cookbook, Yuan Mei showed that he remembered the lessons of Chef Wang. He stressed greater simplicity in cooking. He believed that it was important to bring out the essence of each flavor in the food. Only the freshest ingredients were to be used. Yuan Mei said that selecting food at the market was forty percent of good cooking. "Flavors must be rich and robust, never oily. Those who like greasy food might just as well dine on lard."

With the recipes, Yuan often included humorous comments. One recipe was "Turtle on the Half Shell":

> Remove the head and tail. Braise the meat with seasonings and cover it with its shell. Place one before each guest. How they will fear that it will get up on its legs and walk away!

Yuan Mei continued to pursue the joys of food and poetry till the end of his life. When he was over eighty years old, he reflected on the joys of a long life:

> How few people have lived to see the flowers of four reigns!
> Every moment I am now given comes as a gift from Heaven;
> There is no limit to the glorious things that happen in the
>   spring.
> If you want to call, you need only pause outside the hedge and
>   listen;
> The place from which most laughter comes is certain to be my
>   house!

Anti-Drug Crusader—
Lin Xezu

On March 10, 1839, a flotilla of black boats sailed up the Pearl River to the city of Canton. Golden characters on the sides of the boats announced that they carried a high government official. Those who could not read noticed that the crews wore imperial uniforms—red jackets trimmed with white, and cone-shaped straw hats of the same colors.

Seated on a bed of cushions in one of the boats was a tall, fat man with a thick mustache and a long, scraggly beard. He was Commissioner Lin Xezu, with special orders from the Son of Heaven. His mission: to stop the foreign opium trade that was plaguing China.

About the time when the Chinese stopped their sea voyages, Portuguese sailors were beginning Europe's exploration of the world. In the middle of the sixteenth century, Portuguese merchants arrived in China. Soon they were joined by other Europeans, seeking trade with the world's largest nation. The emperor restricted all foreigners and their trade to Canton, a bustling city in southeast China near the coast.

By the nineteenth century, Great Britain was the leading trading power among the Western nations. Chinese tea, porcelain, and silks were much in demand in the British Isles. But the British produced few goods that China needed and so had to pay for Chinese products with silver. This did not please the British, and they looked around for a trade product that would appeal to the Chinese.

They hit on opium, a drug that was produced in the British colony of India. The growth of the opium trade grew by leaps and bounds, and soon it was China that had to pay with silver. In China drug addiction became a serious problem. It is "a worm that gnaws at our hearts, a ruin to our families," wrote one official, "worse than an invasion of wild beasts."

In 1800 the emperor forbade the importing of opium and other drugs. But many officials had been corrupted, either by their own addiction or by the trade's huge profits. It continued to flourish.

The foreigners who lived at the trade settlement outside Canton watched calmly as Commissioner Lin stepped from his boat. They had bribed or ignored other officials and felt this one would be no different. But the emperor had chosen his representative carefully. Lin was to prove a tough opponent for the foreign drug dealers.

Lin quickly was carried by sedan chair to his *yamen*. After examining the situation, he issued an edict: "Let the Barbarians deliver to me every particle of opium on board their store-ships. There must not be the smallest atom concealed or withheld." He ordered the "barbarians" to sign a pledge never to bring more opium to China. He demanded a response within three days.

The next day, Commissioner Lin forbade any foreigners to leave Canton until the opium issue was settled. In effect, he was holding them hostage. Soon afterward, the leader of the foreign community, the Englishman Charles Elliott, agreed to hand over the opium.

For the next two months, opium was collected and brought to Whampoa, the seaport at the mouth of the river leading to Canton. Commissioner Lin sent men to inspect every ship and warehouse to make sure nothing was held back. By the middle of May, Commissioner Lin had 20,000 chests of opium. He decided to dissolve it in water and then wash it out to sea.

Lin thought it necessary to appease the Spirit of the Southern Sea for polluting the waters. Three days before the destruction, he sacrificed pig bristles, sheep wool, wine, and delicacies to the Spirit, asking her pardon. At the scene of operations, workers dug three trenches inside a bamboo fence. They dumped the opium into the trenches and added salt and lime to make the drug decompose. Then the mixture was flushed into the sea.

Commissioner Lin sent a message to the emperor, reporting the success of his mission. He had reason to feel satisfied. But his troubles were only beginning.

Lin Xezu was born in 1785 at Fuzhou in Fujian Province. He was the son of a scholar who had never been able to pass the highest exams. Lin brought honor to his family by advancing rapidly through the examination system. After passing his Third Degree, he was assigned to the Hanlin Academy. Unlike Yuan Mei, Lin excelled at the study of Manchu language and culture. His knowledge of Manchu prepared him to become one of the emperor's highest officials.

Lin served in a variety of posts and saw firsthand the damage that opium was doing to China. Opium (or "foreign mud," as the Chinese called it) has a soothing effect, but those who smoked it soon became slaves to their habit. In the back alleys of Chinese cities, people slipped into opium parlors and gambling dens to spend hours smoking little pellets in pipes. It weakened them physically and mentally, but its use spread, draining the Chinese economy and bringing more foreign ships loaded down with the addictive drug.

As Governor-General of Hupei and Hunan, Lin devised his own solution. He declared a period of amnesty when all users could turn in their opium, pipes, and supplies without any fear of punishment. But anyone found smoking opium after this period would face severe penalties, even death. Lin had a sure way to tell if a person was an addict. If a prisoner could stand to be in a cell for a day without the drug, Lin freed him.

In 1838 Lin submitted his plan to the imperial government. Impressed, the emperor called Lin to his palace in Beijing. The emperor felt personally disgraced by the drug problem. During one of their conversations, he broke down and wept, saying, "How alas can I die and go to the shades of my Imperial fathers and ancestors, until these dire evils are removed." He named Lin *chin-chai-ta-chin*, or imperial commissioner, giving him the authority to take any means necessary to destroy the trade.

Accompanied by guards, a cook, and servants, Lin left Beijing for Canton. Twenty bearers working in shifts carried his sedan chair. His baggage followed in two large carts. When Lin reached the Yangzi River, he switched to boats. Lin kept a diary. The entry for the first day of the nineteenth year of Tao-kuang's reign (February 14, 1839, in our calendar) read:

> Today at dawn, it being the first of the New Year, I reverently set out an incense-altar on board ship, kowtowed in the direction of the Palace at Peking and wished the Emperor a Happy

New Year. Then I bowed to the shades of my ancestors and made offerings.

As we have seen, Lin was successful in his first efforts to stamp out the drug trade. He then wrote a letter to the young Queen Victoria of Britain. The Chinese had a low opinion of all "barbarian" foreigners. China's emperors had always refused to receive any ambassadors sent from the nations of Europe or America.

But Lin felt that the British queen might respond to a personal appeal. He knew that opium was illegal in her country and so assumed that she knew of its harmful qualities. It seemed to him that if she was informed about the illegal trade, she would take steps to punish her citizens who brought it to China. He wrote her:

> The Way of Heaven is fairness to all; it does not allow us to harm others in order to benefit ourselves. Your country lies twenty thousand leagues away; but for all that, the Way of Heaven holds good for you as for us, and your instincts are not different from ours; for nowhere are there men so blind as not to distinguish between what brings life and what brings death.

It is not known whether this eloquent plea ever reached the queen. But Lin was soon to receive a response from the British that was very different from the one he expected.

After the destruction of the opium on June 23, Commissioner Lin celebrated the birthday of the Chinese god of war. Lin noted in his diary, "After lamps were lit we went to the archery-ground to watch practice with rockets." This celebration was the high point of Lin's career. He had seemingly achieved complete victory over the opium traders. All that remained was to finish the task of stamping out opium-smoking among the people of Canton. But before long, Chinese archers would be pitted against British guns.

In early July, English and American sailors in the Canton area became drunk and got into a brawl with some Chinese citizens. One of the Chinese died from the wounds he suffered. The incident angered Lin, who had also heard that the British were again shipping opium into the port.

Lin demanded that the murderer be turned over to Chinese courts for justice. He added that any new cargoes of opium must also be surrendered. Until these demands were met, Lin ordered that all supplies be cut off from the English families living at

Macao. Macao was a small island near the harbor of Canton which the Portugese had seized in the sixteenth century. Because the Chinese forbade any foreign females from entering the country, the wives and children of the foreign traders lived there.

Captain Elliott began to transfer the traders and their families to British merchant ships. He did not intend to allow Lin to hold British citizens hostage a second time. Elliott also sent a message asking for help from British warships.

As the British withdrew, Commissioner Lin made a visit to Macao. He had never seen many Europeans and Americans before and was not impressed.

> Indeed, they really do look like devils; and when the people of these parts call them "devils" it is no mere empty term of abuse. The foreign women part their hair in the middle, and sometimes even have two partings; they never pile their hair on the top of their head. Their dresses are cut low, exposing their chests, and they wear a double layer of skirt. Marriages are arranged by the young people themselves, not by their families, and people with the same surnames are free to marry one another, which is indeed a barbarous custom.

While Lin was in Macao, two British warships arrived in response to Elliott's message. Elliott boarded one of them and sailed to Kowloon, a few miles north of Canton, intending to ask for supplies. A line of Chinese war junks (small sailing ships) was waiting, blocking the entrance to Kowloon harbor. When the Chinese junks refused to move aside, Captain Elliott gave the order to fire. The Chinese had never before experienced the force of western cannons. The British easily drove the junks away and landed at Kowloon. However, the local Chinese commander sent Lin a false report that the Chinese had scored a victory. Unfortunately, Lin reported this to the emperor without making sure it was correct.

Commissioner Lin really knew little about the outside world. His education in Confucian studies did not prepare him for changing conditions in the world. This ignorance would cost him dearly. For China was no longer the world's most powerful nation. After the Chinese discovery of gunpowder spread to the west, European nations built large cannons that were more powerful than any China possessed. Although Lin had seen British warships, he did not realize their great power. He wrote:

Now here is the reason why people are dazzled by the name of England. Because her vessels are sturdy and her cannons fierce, they call her powerful. Yet they do not know that these vessels are successful only in the outer seas; it is their specialty to break the waves and sail under great winds. If we refrain from fighting with them on the the sea, they have no opportunity to take advantage of their skill.... As to their soldiers, they do not know how to use fists and swords. Also, their legs are firmly bound with cloth and in consequence it is very inconvenient for them to stretch. Should they land it is apparent that they can do little harm.

Not knowing of the Chinese defeat at Kowloon, Lin again wrote Elliott, threatening to destroy the British fleet if the foreigners did not obey his orders. Elliott decided to make another show of force. On November 3, British warships confronted four large Chinese war junks near Canton. They opened fire. In the engagement, the British sank the four junks without any damage to their own ships. After making their naval superiority known, the British withdrew.

Lin realized his mistake, but too late. He bought cannons from the Portuguese at Macao to reinforce the Chinese forts along the coast. He even purchased a ship from the Americans. By now, however, Elliott's reports had reached Britain. Lin was described as a thoroughly evil, greedy official who had "imprisoned" British subjects and unlawfully seized their property (the opium).

The British Parliament voted for war with China. The foreign minister sent a military force to carry a letter to the emperor. The letter complained of Lin's actions and demanded payment for the opium. In addition, it asked the emperor to receive British diplomats at his court and to give up a "large and properly situated island" as a British base.

The next year the British soldiers arrived. Some attacked the coast near Canton. Others landed in the north, driving inland until they were only seventy miles from the capital. From there, they sent on the letter to the emperor.

The emperor, alarmed by having British troops so close to his capital, seized on Lin as a scapegoat. Since the British blamed him for the problem, firing him might satisfy them. On October 13, Lin received the emperor's letter of dismissal. It was insulting. The emperor accused his honest official of

> ...disguising in your dispatches the true state of affairs. You are no better than a wooden image. And as we contemplate your grievous failings, we fall prey to anger and melancholy. Your official seals shall be immediately taken from you and with the speed of flames you shall hasten to Beijing where we will see how you may answer our questions. Respect this! The words of the Emperor.

Before Lin could leave, new instructions arrived. Lin was to stay in Canton to assist the new commissioner. He passed the time writing poetry and doing exercises in calligraphy. His diary betrays no bitterness or regrets. His Confucian philosophy gave him an inner calmness and devotion to duty that supported him in bad times as well as in times of success.

Lin helped prepare the city to defend itself against invasion. Volunteers among the citizens were accepted if they could lift up a heavy spar weighted with granite. Wooden crosses were placed on the walls of the city in the hope that the British soldiers would not fire at them for fear of offending their gods. A plan was hatched to strap firecrackers to monkeys and throw them aboard the British ships to set them afire. The Chinese set their own junks on fire and floated them downstream to harass the British ships.

All this was to no avail. The British were triumphant wherever they attacked. In August 1842 the British and Chinese signed the Treaty of Nanjing. It called for the Chinese to pay an indemnity of $21 million, which included $6 million for the opium Lin had destroyed, referred to as "ransom for the lives of British subjects." China ceded the island of Hong Kong to Britain, opened more ports to British trade, and permitted full diplomatic relations between China and Britain. The only mention of the opium trade in the treaty was the pious hope that smuggling would stop. Of course, the British had no intention of doing so.

Before the treaty was signed, Lin had left Canton in disgrace. He was sentenced to exile in Ili, in the extreme northwestern part of the Chinese Empire. Here, 1,800 years earlier, Ban Chao had pacified China's barbarian enemies. But Lin was too talented to be allowed to remain useless. In 1847, he resumed his official career and served faithfully until his death in 1850.

Lin showed that he had learned from his experience. He wrote to a friend, "Should we not reap great advantage from the superior skill of foreigners? Both the French and Americans brought artisans to Canton who could construct ships; should we not employ European seamen to teach us sailing?" Sadly for China, it had already forgotten the skills that Zheng He had developed.

Despite his failure against the British, Lin is seen as a great hero in today's China. His statue is the first in the Hall of Heroes of the People's Republic. In modern Hong Kong (scheduled to revert to China in 1997), Lin lives again as the hero of movies and stories.

CHAPTER 10

MAKERS OF A NEW CHINA— THE SOONG FAMILY

Sometime before the Chinese New Year of 1888, Charlie Soong stood before an altar in the darkened hold of a junk on the Whangpoo River in Shanghai. The altar stood on a table adorned with long scrolls covered with Chinese characters. Twenty-eight joss sticks (incense) and three red flags stood in a bowl of uncooked rice on the altar.

Charlie Soong was about to be initiated into the Red Gang, one of the Triads, or secret societies of Qing China. Other members of the society had assembled for the ceremony, which was conducted by an Incense Master.

The Incense Master directed Charlie to kneel. One by one, each of the joss sticks was lit. The sweet smell filled the room. The Incense Master handed Charlie some of the sticks. Holding them upside down in both hands, he threw them onto the floor while reciting thirty-six oaths, or pledges, that members made.

The Incense Master held the point of a sword to Charlie's back and asked, "Do you swear loyalty? Do you swear secrecy?" Charlie gave his word. The sword was a reminder of the punishment for violating the oaths: an enforcer would cut his shoulder muscles so that he could never again lift his arms.

Finally, the Incense Master pricked Charlie's finger, mixing the drops of blood into a cup of wine. All present took a sip, and Charlie became their blood brother. He was given a number as a code name and was taught secret hand signals that the members used to recognize each other in public places. Charlie Soong's secret life as a member of the Red Gang had begun.

Secret societies had a long tradition in China. They often arose in times of disorder to overthrow false or unjust rulers. One, called the Red Eyebrows, had worked against Wang Mang, the usurper of the Han Dynasty at the time of Ban Piao. They called themselves

triads after the three forces of the universe: Yang, Yin, and Heaven.

The Red Gang was dedicated to overturning the foreign Manchu Dynasty. In the years since Commissioner Lin and the Opium War, China had endured a "century of shame." China's weakness had enabled Europeans to force ever greater concessions. Shanghai itself was a "treaty port," where foreigners lived in their own sections of the city beyond the reach of Chinese law. Patriotic Chinese wanted to reassert their nation's greatness. As a Red Gang member, Charlie Soong—and later, his children—would change the course of Chinese history.

Charlie Soong was born in 1875 on Hainan Island off the coast of southern China. His father belonged to a great merchant family that had branches throughout Southeast Asia. At the age of nine, Charlie was adopted by an uncle and brought to Boston. In the United States, Charlie's name was Americanized (it was originally Chaio-shun), and he developed a lifelong love of American food, music, and culture. He also became a Methodist Christian and received an education. After running off to sea as a crewman on a revenue cutter catching smugglers, Charlie settled down in North Carolina.

It was here that Charlie met Julian Carr, a tobacco planter and one of the richest men in the United States. Impressed by Charlie's intelligence and determination, Carr sent him to Vanderbilt University. There he trained as a minister, preparing to return to China as a missionary.

Landing in Shanghai in 1886, Charlie found work as a teacher in a Methodist school and started printing Bibles. His students made fun of him because he spoke a southern form of Chinese that was not easily understood in Shanghai. Because he cut his hair short and wore American-style clothes, some Chinese called him "foreign devil." None of this discouraged him.

A Chinese friend whom he had met in the United States introduced Charlie to a young woman named Ni Kwei-tseng. Also a Christian, she had received a good education, excelling in mathematics. But unlike her two older sisters, Kwei-tseng had not attracted a husband. The reason was her big feet. When her mother bound her feet as a child, the girl had developed a high fever. The mother unwrapped the tight bindings, and Kwei-tseng recovered. She never put the bands on again. Even so, her father, a scholar, took pride in his daughter's aptitude for learning. She was also an accomplished pianist. Charlie Soong found her enchanting, and big feet weren't ugly to him. Their wedding took place within a year after he returned to China.

The marriage produced six children, three girls and three boys. Two of the boys later became rich bankers and the other a prime minister of China. The girls would grow up to be China's three most famous women. The Chinese would say of them: "Once upon a time there were three sisters: One loved money, one loved power, one loved China."

The one who loved money was the eldest, Ai-ling ("pleasant mood"). Her father doted on this tomboy of the family, buying her a bicycle for her tenth birthday. No other female in China owned one. Ai-ling and her father turned heads as they cycled together through the streets of Shanghai. She inherited her mother's talent for mathematics and showed early that she had a shrewd head for business. Money never slipped through her fingers.

The one who loved power was the youngest, May-ling ("beautiful mood"). As a child she was chubby and nicknamed "Little Lantern." But she would marry a man who called himself the generalissimo ("all-highest general"), and she helped him to become the most powerful man in China.

The middle girl, the one who loved China, was Ching-ling ("happy mood"). A shy and romantic girl, she grew up to be a beautiful woman who attracted the man known as the George Washington of China, Sun Yat-sen. All three girls attended missionary schools in China and went to the United States for college educations.

With his growing family, Charlie needed a larger income. He concentrated on his printing business and soon dropped out of the ministry. One reason why many ambitious Chinese joined societies such as the Red Gang was that they met influential and powerful business contacts there. Charlie began to print anti-Manchu pamphlets and books that Red Gang members secretly distributed. As he became wealthy, he built an American-style house modeled after the big one on Julian Carr's plantation. He furnished the bedrooms with spring mattresses, an amazing luxury in a country where most people, rich and poor, slept on hard wooden platforms. Charlie also planted coconut palms, just like the ones that grew in his boyhood home, Hainan.

It was through the Red Gang that Charlie met Sun Yat-sen in 1894. Sun and Charlie were much alike. Both were from the south of China, had western educations, and were Christians. Sun had dedicated himself to the overthrow of the Manchus and wanted to create a modern and democratic nation. His rallying cry became, "Expel the Manchus, revive China, establish a republic, and equalize the land." When Sun met Charlie, he found not only a friend, but also a man who could raise money for the cause.

Sun organized many plots against the Manchu government. Some were planned in Charlie Soong's elegant home. But all of them failed. Sun had to flee to the United States, beyond the reach of the Manchu police. Charlie Soong's role in the plots remained a secret from the authorities.

Then, on October 10, 1911, a group of conspirators attacked a government arsenal at Wuhan on the Yangzi River. The soldiers guarding the arsenal came over to the side of the revolutionaries. The revolt spread through the country like wildfire. At the time, Sun was in Colorado raising money for his cause. But he returned to China on Christmas Day and established his headquarters at the Soong house. He sent delegates to all parts of the country, trying to organize the revolution. He soon formed a new government.

Nanjing, upriver from Shanghai, became the capital of the Chinese republic. Sun went there with Charlie and Ai-ling, who had become Sun's personal secretary. Sun's followers thronged the streets of Nanjing, wildly cheering the man who had showed the way to revolution. Delegates from various groups unanimously chose Sun Yat-sen as the first president of the Republic of China.

Sun's first act was to lead a procession to the tombs of the emperors of the Ming Dynasty—the last true Chinese rulers. The blood oaths of the secret society members had included, "Down with the Qing and up with the Ming!" The oath had been fulfilled.

However, the battle was not yet over. Manchu soldiers continued to fight. Then the head of the Manchu army, Yuan Shih-kai, secretly agreed to come over to the rebels' side—if he could be president. Sun agreed to step aside to save the new republic. The last Manchu ruler officially abdicated.

The 1911 revolution was a bold break with the past. The 3,000-

year cycle of dynasties had come to an end. Yet the spirit of absolute rule remained strong. Before long, Yuan Shih-kai showed that he intended to become a dictator. He outlawed Sun's political party, the Guomindang. Sun and many of his followers, including the Soong family, fled to Japan.

While there, Ai-ling met H. H. Kung, a direct descendant of Confucius. The Kung family traced their line back seventy-five generations to the Master. H. H. Kung's great-grandfather, like his illustrious ancestor, had sought a post in government. He studied long and hard to pass the imperial examinations. But the strain was too much. As he sat down to take the test, blood poured from his nose and mouth. He was carried home. Dying, he called for his young son and made him swear "that you will never enter public life, nor ever allow any of our family to do so." That turned out to be good advice, for his sons and grandsons showed a talent for making money. H. H. Kung was a wealthy young man, and before long, he and Ai-ling were married in a Christian ceremony.

Ching-ling, Charlie Soong's middle daughter, took over her sister's duties as Sun's secretary. Without anyone else knowing it, Sun and Ching-ling fell in love.

They were separated when Charlie Soong took his family back to Shanghai. There, Ching-ling shocked her father when she told him she was in love with the much older Sun. He locked her in her bedroom, but her maid brought a ladder to her window during the night. Ching-ling took a boat back to Japan. Charlie rushed after her, but by the time he arrived, Ching-ling and Sun were married.

Charlie confronted his daughter and best friend. A terrible argument followed, and Charlie left, vowing never to speak to either of them again. He returned to Shanghai, telling people that "Ching-ling has formally joined Dr. Sun." Charlie never got over the blow and died a few years later.

After Yuan Shih-kai died in 1916, China fell into chaos. Warlords—powerful generals with their own armies—sliced the country into areas under their personal control. No one was strong enough to establish a national government. Sun set up the headquarters of his Guomindang party in Canton. Although Sun had millions of followers, he needed an army, properly equipped and trained, to unify China. He asked the British and American governments for help, but was turned down.

China's great neighbor to the north, Russia, had experienced its own revolution. A Communist government had taken power in 1917 and renamed the country the Soviet Union. The Soviets offered to send advisers to train Sun's army, and he accepted. In return, Sun agreed to cooperate with the newly formed Chinese Communist Party. Both the Communists and Guomindang shared the goal of a unified China.

Sun and his Communist advisers planned to send their army on a Northern Expedition against the warlords. But Sun died in 1925, before the Northern Expedition began. Ching-ling was left with his papers and their house in Shanghai. Guarding the memory of her husband, Ching-ling became widely respected as the widow of the founder of the Republic of China.

One of Sun's officers, Chiang Kai-shek, became the new leader of the Guomindang. Though he needed the help of the Communists, Chiang secretly plotted to wipe them out. The Northern Expedition proved to be a smashing success. Everywhere, Chinese flocked to the banner of the republic. Chinese Communists in Shanghai organized a strike to help Chiang's forces capture the city. But when Chiang reached Shanghai in the middle of 1927, he ordered his soldiers to attack the Communists. Tens of thousands were slaughtered.

The struggle between the Communists and the Guomindang (later called the Nationalists) split China into two opposing camps. It also divided the Soong family. Ching-ling, Sun's widow, denounced Chiang's action, calling it a betrayal of Sun's ideals. However, Ai-ling and her husband would play important roles in Chiang's government. Chiang proposed to marry the youngest Soong sister, May-ling. He sought the prestige and wealth of the Soong family. May-ling's mother consented to the marriage only after Chiang promised to become a Christian. In December 1927 May-ling became Madame Chiang.

However, a shadow threatened Chiang's power. A group of Communists under the leadership of Mao Zedong still resisted him. Chiang's army surrounded the Communist stronghold, but Mao broke out of the trap. In 1934 and 1935, Mao led his followers on a famous Long March to Shaanxi Province in the northwest. Chiang could not dislodge them.

This fighting had further weakened China, and its neighbor

Japan took advantage. In 1937 Japan invaded China. China proved unable to stop the powerful Japanese army. In December Nanjing fell to an orgy of looting and killing by Japanese troops. Chiang Kai-shek moved his government to Hangzhou, farther up the Yangzi River, but that city too was captured. For the rest of the war, the Chinese government operated at Chongqing, in Sichuan Province. Chiang and the Communists again became allies, united to defend the country against the Japanese threat.

The three Soong sisters were reunited at Chongqing. Under the pressures of war, former quarrels were forgotten. While Japanese planes bombed the city, the famous sisters visited schools and hospitals, offering help to the wounded and dying. They gave speeches to encourage the Chinese to fight on. Movies and phonograph records brought their words to other cities.

After Japan bombed the American base at Pearl Harbor, Hawaii, in December 1941, the United States and China became allies in World War II. Madame Chiang now had an important role to play. She flew to the United States as her husband's goodwill ambassador. Cheering American crowds greeted her, and donations poured in to help China's suffering people. May-ling spoke before a session of Congress, enchanting the Americans with her "long, tight-fitting black gown, the skirt slit almost to the knee."

Another side of May-ling appeared at the White House. As she dined with President Roosevelt and his wife, the president jokingly asked her how she would deal with a coal-miner's strike that had broken out. She silently drew her finger across her neck. Still, she received massive amounts of money for China's defense, although some of it went into the pockets of the Soong family.

The final defeat of Japan in 1945 did not bring peace to China. Civil war once more broke out between the Communists and Chiang's Nationalist government. The Americans continued to send aid to Chiang, but his government became ever more corrupt. After more than three years of fighting, Mao's troops were triumphant. In 1949, he became the head of the People's Republic of China.

Chiang fled with his followers to the island of Taiwan. There he established a government that claimed it would one day retake the mainland. It was a dream that he would never see realized. Madame Chiang was stuck on the other side of the narrow strait that separated Taiwan from China. The "sister who loved power" kept only a shadow of what she wanted. After the death of her husband in 1975, she lived in obscurity in New York City.

Ai-Ling, the "sister who loved money," had magnificent homes in Paris, Hong Kong, and New York City. Limousines took her shopping in the fashionable parts of the world's great cities. She and her husband were billionaires. Charlie Soong's favorite daughter got what she wanted.

And the "sister who loved China?" Ching-ling remained behind when her sisters fled the country. Though Madame Sun was not a Communist, Mao gave her a ceremonial position in his government. She moved back into her father's old house in Shanghai where she had escaped from a bedroom to marry Sun Yat-sen. Perhaps to quiet the ghosts that dwelled within, she adopted two young girls.

Mao became as powerful and cruel as any emperor. He encouraged a "Cultural Revolution," in which young Red Guards attacked anyone suspected of sympathies for the old Chinese ways. Red Guard thugs stormed the Soong house and looted it. Ching-ling escaped harm. Her only comment on the new Communist China was, "We must learn to arm ourselves against ourselves." In 1981 she died of leukemia. The Communist government invited her only surviving sister, Madame Chiang, to the funeral. She refused.

THE SPELLING OF CHINESE NAMES IN ENGLISH

As you know, the Chinese language has its own characters, each representing a different word. Shi Huang Di helped to unify China by making the written Chinese language the same everywhere in China. Unfortunately, writing Chinese names in English is not standardized. This is a problem for anyone beginning to study Chinese history.

For a long time, Chinese names were spelled according to the Wade-Giles system or a modified version of it. In 1979, the Chinese press agency announced a new system, called Pinyin. American newspapers took up the Pinyin system, and most books since then have used it. However, certain names, like China, are so familiar that their old Wade-Giles spellings are kept. (In Pinyin, China would be Qina.)

The Pinyin system uses a Q to represent the sound "ch." It uses an X for the sound "ts" or "z." This makes it awkward for people who don't know the system to pronounce names when reading them aloud. In this book, we have usually followed the Pinyin system, but if you look up some of the people in books published before 1970, you should know how to spell their names in the Wade-Giles system.

PINYIN	WADE-GILES
Ban Zhao	Pan Ch'ao
Ban Chao	Pan Chao
Ban Gu	Pan Ku
Daoism	Taoism
Du Fu	Tu Fu
Gao Zong	Kao Tsung
Guomindang	Kuomintang
Laozi	Lao Tzu
Li Bo	Li Po
Lin Xezu	Lin Tse-hsu
Luoyang	Loyang
Mao Zedong	Mao Tse-tung
Qing (Dynasty)	Ch'ing
Shi Huang Di	Shih Huang Ti
Song (Dynasty)	Sung
Tai Zong	Tai Tsung
Xia (Dynasty)	Hsia
Xian	Sian
Xuan Zong	Hsuan Tsung
Zheng He	Cheng Ho

MAJOR CHINESE DYNASTIES	
Xia (legendary)	c2100 B.C.-c1600 B.C.
Shang	c1700 B.C.-1027 B.C.
Zhou	1027 B.C.-256 B.C.
Qin	221 B.C.-206 B.C.
Han	206 B.C.-A.D. 220
Sui	589-618
Tang	618-907
Song	960-1279
Yuan (Mongol)	1279-1368
Ming	1368-1644
Qing (Manchu)	1644-1912

GLOSSARY

Barbarians: The word Chinese used to describe all non-Chinese, in particular the nomads who lived north and west of the Great Wall.

Buddhism: A religion that spread from India to China. Many Chinese followed Buddhist teachings along with the philosophies of Confucianism and Daoism.

Calligraphy: The art of writing beautifully. Often included as part of a painting.

Concubine: A mistress. It was common for emperors to have many concubines as part of the imperial household.

Confucianism: A philosophy of life first developed by Confucius. It stressed the proper relationships in society, such as father/son and subject/ruler.

Daoism: A philosophy of life founded by Laozi. It drew on nature as a guide.

Dynasty: A family of emperors. The period of time that any family ruled China is known as their dynasty.

Eight-legged Essay: One of the forms required for answers on the imperial examinations. It consisted of eight paragraphs, each developing a specific aspect of the topic.

Examination System: A grueling series of tests that candidates for government posts had to pass to obtain a job.

Foot Binding: The practice of wrapping the feet of female children very tightly so the feet would remain small. It often crippled Chinese women so they could walk only with pain.

Four Treasures: The instruments of writing—paper, brush, inkstone, and ink.

Great Wall: An enormously long masonry wall that the Chinese built to keep out nomadic tribes in the north and west. It was expanded and rebuilt several times in different dynasties.

Guomindang: A political party founded by Sun Yat-sen. Its members later became known as Nationalists.

Hanlin Academy: A college of scholars at the emperor's court. Those who finished highest in the examination system were invited to attend.

Hsieh: A Chinese Robin Hood, a man who took action outside the law to protect the weak and the poor.

Joss Stick: Incense.

Junk: A Chinese sailing ship.

Kowtow: An elaborate ceremony of kneeling and bowing that people used when approaching the emperor's throne.

Li: (1) In Confucian philosophy, correct behavior. (2) A unit of length, about 1/3 of a mile.

Magistrate: A Chinese official similar to a judge, but with the powers of police officer, judge, and jury.

Mandate of Heaven: The emperor's right to rule.

Middle Kingdom: The Chinese name for their country, so called because they believed it was the center of the world.

Opium: An addictive drug that British traders imported to China. Chinese called it "foreign mud," but its use became widespread, with harmful effects on China.

Queue: A braid of hair at the back of the head. The Manchu rulers of the Qing Dynasty required all Chinese males to wear one.

Ren: Benevolence or love, the most important of all virtues in the Confucian system.

Sages: Legendary heroes of Chinese mythology.

Shan-shuei: The Chinese name for landscape paintings, the most popular form of Chinese art. The word means "mountains-water."

Silk Road: A trade route through Central Asia that connected China with the nations farther west.

Son of Heaven: Another term for the Chinese emperor.

Three Great Truths: Buddhism, Confucianism, and Daoism.

Triad: Chinese secret society, often a group dedicated to the overthrow of a false or unjust ruler. Named after the three forces of the universe: Yin, Yang, and Heaven.

Yamen: The headquarters of a local Chinese official.

Yellow Emperor: legendary founder of the Chinese nation.

Yin and Yang: The two opposing forces in the universe, representing principles such as masculine and feminine. Both are equal and necessary for harmony.

BIBLIOGRAPHY

Ayscough, Florence, *Chinese Women Yesterday and Today*, Boston: Houghton Mifflin, 1937.

Birch, Cyril, *Anthology of Chinese Literature*, v. 2, New York: Grove Press, 1972.

Bloodworth, Dennis, *The Chinese Looking Glass*, New York: Dell, 1967.

Bloodworth, Dennis, and Ching Ping, *The Chinese Machiavelli*, New York: Dell, 1976.

Collis, Maurice, *Foreign Mud*, New York: W.W. Norton, 1946.

Cotterell, Arthur, and Morgan, David, *China's Civilization*, New York: Praeger, 1975.

Cotterell, Arthur, *The First Emperor of China*, New York: Holt, Rinehart and Winston, 1981.

Coye, Molly Joel, and Livingston, Jon, eds., *China Yesterday and Today*, New York: Bantam, 1975.

Davis, A.R., *Tu Fu*, New York: Twayne Publishers, 1971.

Dawson, Raymond, *The Chinese Experience*, New York: Scribner's, 1978.

Deacon, Richard, *The Chinese Secret Service*, New York: Ballantine, 1974.

Do-Dinh, Pierre, *Confucius and Chinese Humanism*, New York: Funk and Wagnalls, 1969.

Fitzgerald, C.P., *The Empress Wu*, Vancouver, B.C.: University of British Columbia, 1968.

Franck, Irene M. and Brownstone, David M., *The Silk Road*, New York: Facts on File Publications, 1986.

Gilles, Herbert A., ed., *Gems of Chinese Literature*, New York: Dover Publications, 1965.

Gittings, John, ed., *A Chinese View of China*, New York: Pantheon Books, 1973.

Guisso, R.W.L., and Pagani, Catherine, and Miller, David, *The First Emperor of China*, New York: Birch Lane Press, 1989.

Hahn, Emily, *The Soong Sisters*, Garden City, NY: Doubleday, Doran, 1941.

Hibbert, Christopher, *The Dragon Wakes*, New York: Harper & Row, 1970.

Hoobler, Dorothy and Thomas, *China: History, Culture, Geography*, New York: Globe Books, 1987.

Huntington, Madge, *A Traveler's Guide to Chinese History*, New York: Henry Holt & Co., 1986.

Li, Dun J., *The Ageless Chinese*, 3rd ed., New York: Scribner's, 1978.

Lin, Hsiang Ju, and Lin, Tsui Feng, *Chinese Gastronomy*, New York: Perigee Books, 1969.

Martin, Bernard, *The Strain of Harmony: Men and Women in the History of China*, London, William Heinemann, 1948.

Mirsky, Jeannette, ed., *The Great Chinese Travelers*, Chicago: University of Chicago Press, 1964.

Rugoff, Milton, ed., *The Friends of Marco Polo*, New York: New American Library, 1961.

Seagrave, Sterling, *The Soong Dynasty*, New York: Harper & Row, 1985.

Seeger, Elizabeth, *The Pageant of Chinese History*, New York: David McKay Co., 1967.

Spence, Jonathan D., *The Search for Modern China*, New York: W.W. Norton, 1990.

Swann, Nancy Lee, *Pan Chao: Foremost Woman Scholar of China*, New York: Russell & Russell, 1960.

Waley, Arthur, *The Opium War Through Chinese Eyes*, London: George Allen and Unwin, Ltd. 1958.

Waley, Arthur, *The Poetry and Career of Li Po*, London: George Allen and Unwin, Ltd. 1950.

Waley, Arthur, *Translations from the Chinese*, New York: Vintage Books, 1971.

Waley, Arthur, *Yuan Mei*, London: George Allen and Unwin, Ltd., 1956.

Willetts, William, *Chinese Art*, v. 2, Baltimore, MD: Penguin Books, 1958.

Young, David, translator, *Four T'ang Poets*, Oberlin, Ohio: Field Translation Series, 1980.

S O U R C E S

Chapter 1: Confucius
page 8: "On this excellent..." Do-Dinh, Pierre, Confucius and Chinese Humanism, p. 27.
pages 7-14: Anecdotes about Confucius, Martin, Bernard, The Strain of Harmony: Men and Women in the History of China, pp. 18-20.

Chapter 2: Shi Huang Di
page 15: "the nose of a hornet..." Guisso, R.W.L., and Pagani, Catherine and Miller, David, The First Emperor of China, p. 22.
page 20: "These scholars..." Cotterell, Arthur, and Morgan, David, China's Civilization, p. 153.
pages 20-21: "saying that I lack virtue...." Ibid., p. 154.

Chapter 3: The Ban Family
page 23: "At dawn and at nightfall..." Martin, op. cit., p. 37.
page 26: "If a great man..." Swann, Nancy Lee, Pan Chao: Foremost Woman Scholar of China, p. 28.
page 27: "Only he who penetrates..." Franck, Irene M. and Brownstone, David M., The Silk Road, p. 123.
page 29: "These three ancient customs..." Hoobler, Dorothy and Thomas, China: History, Culture, Geography, p. 89.
page 29: "To teach sons..." Ayscough, Florence, Chinese Women Yesterday and Today, p. 241.

Chapter 4: Empress Wu
page 31: "To be admitted to..." Fitzgerald, C.P., The Empress Wu, p. 3.
page 35: "The Son of Heaven sat..." Ibid., p. 47.
page 35: "Consequently there were informers..." Ibid., p. 115.

Chapter 5: Li Bo and Du Fu
page 38: "Life in the World..." Waley, Arthur, Translations From the Chinese, p. 122.
pages 38-39: "A white horse..." Young, David, Four T'ang Poets, p. 116.
page 39: "For several years..." Waley, Arthur, Li Po, p. 5.
page 41: "Forever committed..." Hoobler, op. cit., p. 97.
page 42: "On Boiled Rice Mountain..." Young, David, op. cit., p. 56.
page 42: "I remember in..." Davis, A.R., Tu Fu, p. 17.
page 43: "Three nights in a row..." Young, David, op. cit., pp. 96-7.
page 44: "I suddenly thought..." Davis, A.R., op. cit., p. 27.
pages 44-45: "Women like goddesses..." Young, David, op. cit., pp. 85-7.
pages 45-46: "Hand to hand..." Ibid., pp. 61-3.
page 46: "Tonight..." Ibid., p. 98.

Chapter 6: Ma Yuan
page 47: "When I return..." Cotterell and Morgan, op. cit., p. 129.
page 49: "Every horizontal stroke..." Hoobler, op. cit., p. 40.
page 50: "Grasp the brush..." Willetts, William, Chinese Art, pp. 553-4.
pages 51-52: "It is human nature..." Cotterell and Morgan, op. cit., p. 131.

Chapter 7: Zheng He
page 54: "We have beheld..." Coye, Molly Joel, and Livingston, Jon, China Yesterday and Today, pp. 84-5.
page 56: "In dark weather..." Bloodworth, Dennis, The Chinese Looking Glass, p. 204.
page 57: "The ships which sail..." Mirsky, Jeannette, The Great Chinese Travelers, p. 242.
page 60: "Its inhabitants live..." Ibid., p. 253.
page 60: "do not venture..." Ibid., p. 254.

Chapter 8: Yuan Mei
page 62: "Cooking is like matrimony..." Bloodworth, op. cit., p. 244.
page 63: "when I was cold..." Waley, Arthur, Yuan Mei, p. 10.
pages 66-67: Quotes about and by Chef Wang, Ibid., pp. 52-3
page 69: "One day a guest said..." Ibid., p. 196.
page 69: "Remove the head and tail..." Lin, Hsiang Ju, and Lin, Tsui Feng, Chinese Gastronomy, p. 45.
page 69: "How few people..." Waley, op. cit., p. 198.

Chapter 9: Lin Xezu
page 72: "Let the Barbarians deliver..." Collis, Maurice, Foreign Mud, pp. 201-202.
page 73: "How alas can I die..." Hibbert, Christopher, The Dragon Wakes, p. 112.
pages 73-74: "Today at dawn..." Waley, Arthur, The Opium War, p. 16.
page 74: "The Way of Heaven is fairness..." Gittings, John, A Chinese View of China, p. 45.
page 75: "Indeed, they really do..." Waley, The Opium War, pp. 68-69.
page 76: "Now here is the reason..." Collis, op. cit., p. 180.
page 77: "disguising in your dispatches..." Hibbert, op. cit., p. 152.
page 78: "Should we not..." Ibid., p. 378.

Chapter 10: The Soong Family
page 84: "that you will never enter public life..." Hahn, Emily, The Soong Sisters, p. 38.
page 84: "Ching-ling has formally..." Seagrave, Sterling, The Soong Dynasty, p. 138.
page 86: "long, tight-fitting..." Hahn, op. cit., p. 385.
page 87: "We must learn to arm..." Seagrave, op. cit., p. 461.

INDEX

It is customary for Chinese names to be written with the family name, or surname, first. This book has followed that practice. Thus, to find page references for the poet Li Bo, you would look under Li, not under Bo. Exceptions have been made for Chinese names that have been "westernized," as for example Charlie Soong and his daughters, the Soong sisters.